Hold Fast

FINDING FAITH IN A GOOD GOD ON A JOURNEY ACROSS THE SEA

KELLIE COVERT

Copyright © 2022 by Kellie Covert.

Published by Kellie Covert.

All rights reserved. No part of this publication may be reproduced, distributed, or transmitted in any form or by any means, including photocopying, recording, or other electronic or mechanical methods, without the prior written permission of the publisher, except in the case of brief quotations embodied in critical reviews and certain other non-commercial uses permitted by copyright law.

Scriptures taken from the Holy Bible, New International Version®. Copyright © 1973, 1978, 1984, by International Bible Society. Used by permission of Zondervan. All rights reserved worldwide. www.zondervan.com. The 'NIV' and 'New International Version' are trademarks registered in the United States Patent and Trademark Office by International Bible Society.

Table of Contents

Preface 7

Part 1: TO SOMETHING NEW 9
    Attainable 10
    Beginnings 12
    Do You Know What We Did Today? 18
    I Want You to Dream 24
    Will You Consider? 27
    Moving Forward 30
    STCW 34
    No New Nuts 39
    Leaving Isle of Wight 43
    The Burger Incident 48
    Into Jersey 53
    Sail to Cardiff 57
    Sail to Glasgow 60
    Stuck in Glasgow 63
    Dinghy Training 65
    Running Through Puddles 67
    No Longer Detained 70
    Coming into Liverpool 74
    Our Stories 78
    To Something New 80

Part 2: TO SEE AND KNOW 83
    To See and Know 84
    Thanks to an Irishman 86
    Stuck in Birkenhead 88
    Running at Sea Level 93
    Status of the Heads 96

Glowing Dolphins 99
Tying the Sail..104
Engine Checks 107
Constellations... 112
The Life Jacket 115
Melodies 118
Don't Give Up on the First Watch 120
A Week at Sea..123
Thanksgiving...127
Orion 132

Part 3: TO FEEL HIS ABSENCE 139
Surviving the Squall 140
Stuck at Anchor...148
Eating in Foreign Countries... 155
This Is Where I Have You 160
Bean Warriors 164
Rigging the Mizzen... 167
Anchor Watches 169
Heave To 172
In Paphos 175
MOB 179
Jerusalem 183
Outside Watch...189
Bike Adventures 191
Turkey – England 194
Where Were You? 198
End on a Good One 1201

Part 4: TO HIS REDEMPTION 205
Back in Gozo...207
On Seasickness 212

Dry Dock 217
In Pieces 222
Sea Shanty Night 229
Thunderstorms Roll In 231
Shley on the Mainsail.. 238
Knowing Your Home 241
Unfortunate Arrival 244
Losing to the Sea 253
Pumpkin 260
Give Me Something to Say 267
By the Breakwater 269

Part 5: TO GRATITUDE 273
The Last Sail...275
The Nickey Line 281
Remembering a Yes 285
Guiding Hand of a Loving God 287

Epilogue...293

Acknowledgements 297

About the Artist..301

For Kenzi

*May your life always be full of wonder, joy and adventure.
Love you.*

Preface

Writing this book has been no easy feat. These stories have been stored on my computer for years. I kept trying to find the perfect moment of inspiration to get it all done while secretly hoping it would just happen one day and the book would magically be in my hands. If only life worked that way ever.

I struggled to even begin the process of putting these stories in place. I was trying to write a long narrative of every single detail of my life on a boat. That's like asking you to think back and tell me everything you did for every single day of second grade. Not gonna happen.

What you have in your hands is not a narrative or a novel. This isn't a tale of a missionary journey. I would hardly even claim it as a memoir. It is by no means exhaustive of everything I experienced living on a boat. It only covers a fraction of it. And it's most definitely not the full account of the ministry of Youth with a Mission (YWAM) S/Y[1] Next Wave, a story which could be told by a few other people far better than I ever could, and I hope one day they actually do that because it has a pretty incredible history.

This is simply a collection of stories. Stories that make up a greater story. The good and the ugly stories. The stories of adventures and seemingly mundane moments. The calm seas and stormy gales. It's a story of finding faith in a good God during some of the most epic and challenging years of my life.

A story that is sometimes hard to believe is mine.

---

[1] S/Y is an abbreviation for *sailing yacht*.

Part 1
TO SOMETHING NEW

October 2012 – December 2012

Isle of Wight, England – Jersey, Channel Islands: 2 days, 132 nm
Jersey, Channel Islands – Cardiff, Wales: 2 days, 291 nm
Cardiff, Wales – Glasgow, Scotland: 3 days, 371 nm
Glasgow, Scotland – Liverpool, England: 2 days, 220 nm

Attainable

The blank canvas stares me in the face.

So many possibilities, so much potential. Where does it even begin?

It begins with an idea.

Now, I'm no scientist, and I don't know exactly how the brain works. But somewhere in this *constant flow* of neurons and other electric currents that sends signals to my legs to make them *walk*, my arms to make them *embrace*, my heart to make it *beat*, the smallest of charges makes its way to a certain part of my brain – which sparks an idea. Here it begins to grow and take shape into something.

SOMETHING.

Something new, something different, something uniquely designed, something original. Something *attainable*.

It is this something that awakens the desire to transform this seemingly unattainable possibility into a tangible reality.

The blank canvas stares me in the face.

I've never been a big dreamer. Sure, I've had an imagination where I would conjure up stories and songs and scenarios of something outside myself. But somewhere, my imagination became just that – *imaginary*. Not real, not possible, nonexistent. So why begin to dream? Why put me through the joy and excitement of those dreams only to be disappointed by the realisation that it would never happen?

The blank canvas stares me in the face.

But once again, this long-lost neuron charges its way from the cells in my brain to the *depths* of my heart then back to that one place that sparks this idea, this imagination, this dream, this desire. The possibilities of what could be go rushing through my head.

This time it's different. This time there is *hope* in these possibilities. Hope in these dreams.

A hope assuring me that this *awakened desire* of what could be, can be, and will be.

Beginnings

The basic premise of biblical trust is the conviction that God wants us to grow, to unfold, and to experience the fullness of life.

Brennan Manning, Ruthless Trust

Looking back at what has brought you to where you are today, the good and the bad, the ordinary and extraordinary, the steady and uncomfortable, the triumphs and trials, what if you saw *all* of those as invitations?

What if you discovered that in every season of life, you were being invited into something? Something good. Something meaningful. Something you hadn't thought of before.

What if it was God doing the inviting?

And what if you said yes to God's invitations?

They don't always look like an elaborately addressed envelope in your mailbox with a beautifully hand-written letter inside. In fact, most of them don't. Probably none of them. Most of the time, they look like completely ordinary things. Some of them might even look like failures to you.

But what if you could see them all as God's invitations?

This is the story of my saying yes.

One day a man named Jack asked me a question. We were walking down to one of my favourite pubs in Harpenden, England, called Inn on the Green, to have a pint.

He asked, 'Can you tell me all the places in the world you've been to so far?'

Starting from the most recent and working backwards, I started listing every place I'd been privileged enough to travel to during my relatively short life. Then there were the places I would be going to in the coming year. As my list grew longer, his eyes grew wider with intrigue.

When I finished, he joked, 'You know, I think you need to get out more.'

It was at that moment I suddenly had a desire to write my stories.

I have enjoyed writing ever since I was a kid. I always thought I was pretty good at it too. I still have a red folder of writing pieces from sixth grade somewhere in a box of old things that I'm still rather proud of. Though I guess you'll be the judge of my writing abilities now. Hopefully, they've improved from my ten-year-old self. Writing has always been my way of processing things, of getting things outside of my overthinking, Enneagram One mind. They ranged from poetic types to essays of sorts. Most being reflective, simple and meaningful, others just informational. I have stacks of journals recounting important moments in my life. I've always had some desire to write in one form or another.

This desire felt different though.

This time, I wanted to write to remember every part of the crazy journey I was on.

I didn't want to forget what my life had become. It was purely selfish.

———⟨⟨———

In January 2011, I first stepped foot on English soil and my life would never be the same. Cliché as that is, it's true. I was twenty-one years old and had absolutely no idea what to do with my life.

Not even a faint idea. When the opportunity presented itself to spend six months in another country focused solely on my relationship with God while living in community with others, promising missions and lots of travelling, it was not a hard sell.

I started doing my research on what Youth with a Mission (YWAM) was all about and what the heck a Discipleship Training School (DTS) was. The more information I took in, the more intrigued I became. The idea of going somewhere to jump a program involving three months of teachings and then three months of outreach, putting what was learned into practice, sparked something inside of me. I desperately wanted to be part of it. I hadn't felt that way for a long time. My heart raced at the thought of such an outrageous possibility.

I immediately knew I wanted to go to England. I didn't even consider any other countries. My mom was born in Sunderland, England and her family moved to the US when she was young. England felt a part of me despite never seeing it with my own eyes. I grew up on Sunday roasts at Grandma and Grandpa Bristow's house after church, consuming endless amounts of Yorkshire Puddings, Jelly Babies and Refreshers. Their English accents were just normal to me. I can picture the placemats on the small table in the kitchen filled with scenes from around Sunderland. Old family photos have been engrained in my mind from looking through the very detailed Bristow Chronicles Grandpa compiled. I was anxious for a chance to see it for real.

The English countryside beckoned as I perused through the multiple locations of YWAM locations across England. I ended up on YWAM Harpenden's website located on a gorgeous piece of land called Highfield Oval (more often referred to as just, The Oval). I spent hours upon hours looking through every bit of information I could find, watching every video and scrolling through every picture. Beautiful old buildings were set around a huge oval field lined with trees. The thought of being able to live in a place like that was something I never thought I was allowed to dream of.

I'm embarrassed to admit what almost kept me from submitting my application to do my DTS in England. But here we go. I tend to overthink most things in my life on a very regular basis. It's not my favourite quality. My heart knew I was ready and excited for this adventure, but my mind told me otherwise.

There were two incredibly simple tasks I had to complete before being able to go that I just didn't want to do. I would have to go to a doctor for a basic medical check-up and go through the process of getting a visa. That's it. Ridiculous, right? It was as simple as making a phone call and filling out paperwork. I wasn't even worried at the thought of travelling to a new country I'd never been where I didn't know anyone. Nope, I just didn't want to put the effort in to get fingerprinted for a visa. Thank the good Lord for Uncle Ed who, in much kinder words, said I would be pretty stupid to be hindered by something as insignificant as a few logistics. His kinder words included that if I was faithful to God in walking in the direction I felt he was leading, he would be faithful in helping me get there.

I filled out my DTS application and anxiously waited for the next month to finally see one word: Accepted.

It was happening. This was real. I could hardly believe it.

I was going to England.

That statement alone sent excitement through me like wildfire.

A couple months later, with visa and plane ticket in hand, I boarded the plane with disbelief at the ridiculous turn my life had suddenly taken. I was on a plane by myself crossing over the Atlantic Ocean to arrive in a country I had never been to, knowing absolutely no one on the other side. I watched a video about how to get through Heathrow Airport about four times before landing so I wouldn't look like a lost tourist and could find my way. I was just hoping I could easily find someone with a sign indicating they were with YWAM. I saw it right when I walked out the arrival doors and nervously walked in that direction towards the person who would be the first to welcome me to England.

I had no idea what was ahead of me.

A few months after that pint at Inn on the Green with Jack in Harpenden, I had over 100 pages written. I kept writing because I wanted to be sure to get every single detail right so I could remember it all perfectly. I loved writing every story and started seeing so much good in everything. It got me more excited for the life I was living. The possibility of writing a book one day was somewhere in the back of my mind, but that's where it stayed for a while.

My crazy, four-and-a-half-year adventure in Europe came to an end not long after my story writing began. The kinds of stories I was living suddenly stopped being my normal. I moved back home to Colorado, and my life was drastically different. Readjusting to life outside of a mission's lifestyle community is hard. Really hard. If you've ever done it, you can understand in one way or another. But my life didn't feel as exciting anymore, and I was kind of crushed by that for a little while.

So, I stopped writing.

It hurt to write. It hurt to tell my stories. It hurt to even think about them. No one around me could relate or understand. I missed it all too much.

But it also hurt not to write. It hurt not to tell my stories. Not to remember. I was scared I'd start forgetting.

Years went by, and the book idea faded to a distant dream. But that's the thing about our heart's desires. There's always a reason for them, either immediately or years from when they first surface. Enough time had passed that I was able to look back on my stories with a smile on my face and gratitude in my heart.

Then, one day a friend named Amanda was listening to me tell her my favourite story about glowing dolphins as we sat outside a café in the Colorado mountains enjoying a cup of tea. As memories came up throughout our conversation and how it still related to my life, she smiled.

She said, 'Kellie, people need to hear your stories.'

It was at that moment the desire surfaced again to write them.

And not just for me this time. But for you.

So, here's to remembering. And here's to you.

Do You Know What We Did Today?

DATE: April 2012
LOCATION: Liverpool, England
53° 24' 5.9" N
2° 59' 32.4" W

After being a student on the January 2011 DTS, I felt it on my heart to continue being a part of YWAM and to staff the following January 2012 DTS. I wanted to keep going with what God was doing in my life and England just felt like home. It also happened to be during the Summer Olympics in London, so I really wanted to be around for that because that sounded awesome.

I had a week off quickly approaching in April 2012, and I was looking forward to heading up to Newcastle to see a favourite city again and some familiar faces. That didn't end up happening though. Something far greater did.

I had recently met a few people who were crew members on board S/Y Next Wave, a forty-two-metre sailing yacht. It was a floating YWAM base. I had mentioned my predicament to these few people of not knowing where to go for my upcoming week off since my original plans had fallen through. They enthusiastically invited me to come visit them on the ship which was then docked in Liverpool. Even with my limited knowledge of this ship, it didn't take me long to realise how great of an idea that was. I had seen pictures and heard stories about Next Wave but didn't think much of it at the time. I never thought I would actually see it in person. It felt so distant. It was another thing I didn't think I was allowed to dream of.

I quickly sent an email to the ship's directors, Daniel and Tamara, introducing myself and expressing interest in staying on board for a couple days that upcoming weekend. I knew it was incredibly last-minute, and they had absolutely no idea who I was, but surprisingly, they said yes. I hopped online to purchase a MegaBus ticket, and a week later, I made my way to London to begin the seven-hour journey by coach north to Liverpool One bus station.

When I got off the coach in Liverpool, a crew member came to meet me and walked me back through the heart of Liverpool towards Royal Albert Dock to find the ship right at the entrance to this historic spot. Excited was too vague a word.

I carefully walked across the metal steps of the gangway[2] with a green net on either side and boarded the ship for the first time. I got a tour of the whole ship. It had three decks. The lowest deck housed most of the cabins (where I'd be staying those few days in a small cabin with a couple other girls. I would soon realise how little headspace I would soon be having in that bunk), the engine room, electrical closet and a bathroom containing a shower affectionately known as the love shower … It had two shower heads and a curtain in the middle but that is still how everyone referred to it. Making my way up to the next deck at the front, we passed by the skansen[3] where we'd later watch a movie. That stairway led passed a few bathrooms and through a set of swinging doors leading into the main saloon

---

2   A moveable walkway to get from ship to shore.
3   The skansen is what we called the forward most room of the ship. It was our library/meeting room/storage/spare cabin/extra bathroom/movie theatre. The word "skansen" comes from the Swedish word, "skans" which means "forecastle" (forecastle meaning the forward most room on a ship). With Next Wave having been built in Sweden, this made sense to use a Swedish word. Though I guess the extra 'en' was just kind of thrown on the end of the word to become what we so lovingly referred to it as.

with a skylight above us. This was the main area of the ship full of benches and tables and cupboards full of food and tea and coffee and dishware with a big whiteboard on the wall that had something new drawn on it every day, mostly schedules but seemed like a place people could get creative. Going through the saloon, I came to the galley[4] where people were already cooking the next meal. Then there was the hallway called the hall of fame containing photos from every team and crew over the years which was right next to the hall that led to a few crew cabins and another tiny bathroom. Going up another set of stairs brought us to the wheelhouse[5] which is where all the magic happened. There were buttons and lights and gadgets and gauges and torpedo buttons. There was the radar, navigational computer, GPS, radio and just all the sailing things. Behind that was the Navigation office with a desk, a bench and dropdown table to have space to map out a course. Behind that was the captain's cabin. Going back outside to the main deck, I was surrounded by ropes and all types of rigging all around. The boat had two masts and five sails. There was a small dinghy hanging off the back and out front was a huge long pole with a rope underneath begging to be climbed. Also begging to be climbed was the forward mast up to the crow's nest but I'll get to that.

Instantly, I was welcomed into the community and felt right at home. At dinner, they asked me to grab a piece of paper with a question on it from a hat. A question I had to answer about myself. I don't remember the question, but it just made me feel like I somehow had a place there. I was seen, noticed, welcomed and people were interested in getting to know me despite my being there for only four days. We watched a movie later in the

---
4   A ship's kitchen.
5   The part of the ship that housed the steering wheel and all other navigational equipment.

skansen with my famous peanut butter popcorn in a big bowl. I helped out where I could those few days, jumping into meal preps and clean-ups and morning workouts and just getting to know the amazing crew members from all over the world who lived on board.

The next day, I went around the city with another crew member, and we explored the free museums, charity shops and the main city centre. I quickly decided that Liverpool was going to be one of my favourite cities. Returning back to the ship, I harnessed up and climbed the ratlines[6] up to the crow's nest[7]. Climbing up and around the platform took some awkward manoeuvring, but hoisting myself up offered incredible views of Albert Dock, Liverpool Cathedral up on the hill in the distance and the Museum of Liverpool across the dock with the Liver Building just beyond it, all right next to the River Mersey. Looking below, I had the best bird's eye view of the deck of Next Wave and all its riggings reaching up to me and beyond.

It was someone's birthday that night, and I was first introduced to a Next Wave birthday tradition. The birthday person was asked two simple questions: What were some major highlights from the last year, and what were they most looking forward to in the coming year? After those questions were answered, the rest of the crew on board took the time to encourage them and talk them up. Then, there was always a delicious dessert. These people really cared and liked each other.

A small group of us awoke very early the next day to embark on what would turn into quite the adventure. The original intent

---

6   Lines tied between shrouds (parts of the rigging that hold up the mast) to make a ladder.
7   A platform near the top of the mast as a place for a lookout.

was to drive two hours up to the beautiful Lake District (a gorgeous place known for its lakes, forests and mountains) to have a picnic by the water. We found the perfect spot, brought out our blanket and picnic basket, and enjoyed a lovely lunch, while also attempting to climb the tree we sat under.

Midday came, and the question arose of what to do next. I'm not sure who suggested this, but an idea was thrown out about carrying on up to Scotland. Edinburgh, to be exact. Another three hours north. It was met with a unanimous yes.

On we drove up to Edinburgh. We stopped a couple times on the side of the motorway, once to take a picture of the 'Welcome to Scotland' sign, another to look at sheep and woolly cows. We made it to our destination, and I was in awe of the city as we drove through the winding cobblestone streets with its amazing architecture of the surrounding buildings. We wandered up to Edinburgh Castle but arrived too late to be able to go in. However, we did manage to make it in time to watch the sunset on top of the hill. Which was beautiful.

We decided dinner was important so, of course, I had haggis. I was in Scotland, so it felt necessary. This was my second attempt at having haggis and, like the first, it was a success. It's not as bad as some may think, once you get past what it actually is. Especially when paired with neeps and tatties (turnip and potatoes).

One of my favourite conversation starters on this adventure was this question:

'Do you know what we did today?'

We asked a lot of people that question and this was usually the reply:

'No, what?'

'Well, we left from a ship, which we live on, docked in Liverpool and drove to the Lake District to have a picnic lunch.

Then, we decided to keep driving, so we came all the way up here to Edinburgh. And now we are going to drive back to Liverpool tonight.'

'Wow.'

'I know!'

After haggis came the long, terrifyingly fast drive back south to Liverpool. We managed to make it back by midnight. We covered a lot of miles in a lot of hours that day. The rest of the crew had wondered all day about what we had gotten up to, especially when we arrived so late.

But I realised, that's the kind of place this ship was. The kind where you go off on ridiculous adventures when you have a day off with people you just met. The kind where people wonder where you are, wanting to be sure you make it home safe.

The kind that often found themselves asking, 'Do you know what we did today?'

I Want You to Dream

DATE: *April 2012*
LOCATION: *Liverpool, England*
  53° 24' 5.9" N
  2° 59' 32.4" W

I have never been a big dreamer. I was never one of those people who knew exactly what they wanted to do with their life and then just did it. I've always taken things as they come. It's worked out pretty well for me so far. But when I was on Next Wave for the first time, I heard so many sailing stories from everyone, and something hit me. They were living in such a way that I had never seen before, never thought possible. It was new and exciting and freaking cool.

I went to the grocery store with Daniel one afternoon to help shop for that week's food. He very purposefully walked through the aisles of Tesco like he had done it a hundred times (which he definitely had), grabbing everything he needed while simultaneously telling me about what it was like to live on Next Wave as well as asking me about the kind of leader I wanted to be and what I was good at. He asked me what I was hoping for in the future. It kind of felt like an interview. He told me about the kind of leaders he and his wife, Tamara, were as directors of the ship. He told me about the purpose and mission of Next Wave. Through our conversation, interspersed with picking out meat, cereals and tea, something sparked in me again at the possibility of what my life could be, and I couldn't help but smile.

With two shopping carts full to the brim and then some of food, we loaded everything onto the floor of the taxi and headed back to Albert Dock. Upon arrival, Daniel yelled down for a grocery chain. Everyone dropped what they were doing and formed a line from the galley up to the gangway to help get all the food on board.

That night, as I was lying in my bunk, I was posed with an invitation from God:

'I want you to dream.'

Every conversation had, every story heard, just being on the boat, awakened a desire in me for something more. It challenged me to think bigger for my life. So, when posed with this invitation, I decided that the next day, I would start dreaming. I would write a list of all the things I wanted to do: big things, small things, medium things. I went to sleep excited to wake up early the next morning.

Sitting at a café in Waterstone's with my tie-dye tape-covered notebook, I started writing my list. Some things I knew could happen in the near future, some, I thought, were a lot less likely. I wrote that I wanted to go to Salzburg and go on some kind of *Sound of Music* tour, I wanted to draw and paint more, I wanted to write a song, and I wanted to sail on Next Wave. I wrote down everything that came to my mind no matter how plausible it was. For me, as a very practical, realistic, everything has to be right and possible, person, this was a big deal to not be bound by my own thinking of impossibility.

I put my pen down to look at my list, satisfied with what was on there, trusting there was a reason God asked me to dream. Hoping this was an invitation to something new and exciting.

The next night, as I turned the lights off to go to sleep, another invitation:

'Why not staff the September DTS?'

This came as a bit of a surprise as I hadn't thought I would want to staff another DTS, especially one that started less than a month after the current one I was already staffing was to end. I was at the beginning of a two-year commitment to YWAM Harpenden but after that DTS, the future was uncertain.

The more I thought about the question, the more I knew it was from God and that I actually really wanted to do it. So, I tucked that thought away to consider later.

I was sad when the time came to get back on a bus to Harpenden after those four days on a boat, but I was sure this was the start of some kind of relationship with Next Wave and its awesome crew. And I was pretty happy about that.

Those few days left a mark and would truly change the trajectory of my entire life. I just didn't know it then.

Will You Consider?

DATE: April 2012
LOCATION: Harpenden, England
      51° 49' 32.1" N
      0° 21' 35.9" W

> *We pray, 'Lord, I'll go wherever you want me to go.' Then we sit in a car with the gear in neutral and our hands locked on the steering wheel, waiting for further instructions. A few times in Scripture, God speaks to people when they're in this position. But most of the time he meets them along the way and redirects them.*
>
> *They were all doing something. Then God stepped in and radically changed their course.*
>
> Holley Gerth, You're Made for a God-Sized Dream

A week or so after that unexpected trip to visit a boat in Liverpool, I was sitting in The Oval Café across from my very good friend and mentor, Jessica. I was talking to her all about my adventure on Next Wave. I told her about my dream list, I told her about God inviting me to consider staffing another DTS that September, I told her about how good everything was.

Then, she asked me a question that caught me off guard.

'Will you consider staffing the September DTS *on Next Wave?*'

She was asking me to consider going to spend six months on a sailboat. To consider becoming a freaking sailor. Shocked, I asked where this came from.

'Well, they need another girl to staff the school, and someone recommended you.'

Hearing this, I froze with a big, stupid grin on my face.

'What? Really? I could do that? Ha!'

In Exodus 3, Moses was shepherding when he stumbled upon the burning bush. He was going about his life, doing his thing, when God stepped in and radically changed his life, his purpose, his direction.

In Matthew 4, Simon and his brother, Andrew, were fishing when Jesus called them to follow Him. They were doing their normal, everyday job when Jesus stepped in and radically changed their lives, purpose and direction.

Neither of their lives was wrong from the start when God stepped in. But God had something bigger, something better for their lives that he was so excited to invite them into. But their lives were changed because they said yes. They said yes to something new, something different, something only God could bring together, something only God could come up with.

They said yes to God's invitation.

I told Jessica I would pray about this outrageous opportunity, but I didn't think I needed to. I was so excited at the possibility of what I could get to do. Plus, I already had my heart set on staffing another DTS anyway, so why not just switch locations?

I did what I said and I prayed about it, and the more I prayed and considered it, the more I knew that was the way I should go. And the way I wanted to go. It was something I really wanted to be part of. I wanted to work with that crew, I wanted to learn to sail, I wanted to grow in my giftings, I wanted to continue to become the leader God had made me to be, and this was a great opportunity to be thrown into it. I needed to be challenged, and here was the perfect path for that. I was eager and ready.

Three weeks after my initial visit, three weeks after having an unforgettable four days with people I didn't know on a freaking boat in Liverpool, I sent an email to them saying I was interested in staffing their upcoming DTS. Just three weeks after getting a small taste of Next Wave, I unexpectedly was up for committing six months of my life to do this crazy thing. For some reason, they accepted my offer after having no real idea who I was apart from the recommendation of one person and a very brief introduction.

Moving Forward

DATE: September 2012
LOCATION: Harpenden, England
      51° 49' 32.1" N
      0° 21' 35.9" W

Transition. A word that used to mean so very little to me but then was all I could think about. Transitions always seem to come during the moments you least want them to. But they come, ready or not. And you just have to brave the waves of emotions that come along with it. To transition is not just simply to move on. It's to move ahead, to move forward. For some, that seems quite exciting, and at times in my life, it was exciting. But for others (and myself one moment at one o'clock in the morning), it's nothing more than a time when emotions are high and tears flood down the cheeks and everything feels out of control.

    Transitions are the times between what is and has been known and lived, to what is unknown and yet to be lived. A time when things change. It's when a lot of things change and, annoyingly, all at once. Relationships, living spaces, surroundings, beds, sunsets, homes. Transitions are hard no matter how excited you are about what's coming next.

    My question at that moment in the middle of the night: Could I continue what had been lived, to what was yet to be lived? This person that had been, to this person that would be? The friends I was surrounded by, to the friends yet to meet?

———←←———

I'm not always one to remember exactly when and how a friend became a friend. A lot of times it feels like all of a sudden, there we are, conversing as friends, and I had no idea what started it all. For some reason, recollection of that first encounter just flies out of my memory. I have a small handful of exceptions, but for the most part, the very beginnings of friendships don't really have a secure home in my brain.

Here's one exception though.

It was about a week before I was going to be moving my life from land to water, from countryside to seaside. I didn't quite know what to expect, and my emotions were all over the place. All I knew was that I was going to be moving into a very small space with twenty other people from all over the world whom I didn't know while attempting to learn things I had never done before.

One of those twenty people happened to be someone named Tamara.

I had a very brief encounter with her that first time I was on Next Wave, but she was quite sick those few days, so I hardly saw her, let alone had a real conversation with her. But even then, I knew she was just really cool, and I wanted to be cool like her and with her. So, I nervously sent her a short message asking if we could get together. I figured since we were going to soon be living and working very closely together, we should probably get to know one another. To my relief, she agreed.

We sat with our drinks at The Oval Café telling each other our stories. She told me what it was like to live on a ship, what we would be doing, and where we would be going. Just talking to her and getting to know her got me so excited for what I would soon be jumping into. I knew even more clearly it was exactly where God wanted me to be, the direction he wanted me to be heading, despite everything about that direction being completely unknown and uncertain. And a little crazy.

I told her how I had been praying about what strengths I thought I could bring to the ship. The main thing was worship. Worship leading was something God had been growing in me the previous months and years and something I was really excited to keep exploring. What was significant about this was that a worship leader was a role needing to be filled in the community. Hearing that was even more confirmation that it was exactly where God wanted me to go. He had given me a heart for something, and he led me to a place where I would be able to use that gift where it was needed.

Nearing the end of our conversation, she asked me a very simple question.

'Kellie? Will you be my friend?'

'Yes! Will you be my friend?'

'Yes!'

Now, we were both in our mid-twenties as we asked each other this very elementary question. But since when is that question only supposed to be asked among five-year-olds?

―――― ≪ ≪ ――――

I continued to fight my body's natural urge to go to sleep as I sat outside on the small balcony of upstairs building number four at two o'clock in the morning. My eyes were so tired and heavy, but they didn't want to close. They wanted to capture and hold onto what had been lived. I didn't want to let it go, to let it out of my sight. But I knew I had to.

I couldn't keep my eyes open anymore, so I gave in. I went inside, climbed into my bed, and closed my eyes, knowing that everything was going to be different when I woke up the next morning. The next morning, I would be moving to a boat.

The thing I've come to learn about transitions is that you have no idea the good that is ahead of you. All you know is the good you're leaving behind. And it hurts. A lot. But there's also this knowing that it's necessary, that moving forward is good and for your best.

STCW

DATE: September 2012
LOCATION: Cowes, Isle of Wight, England
  50° 45' 35.7" N
  1° 17' 34.7" W

One month before I would be making the journey to the Isle of Wight to join the crew of S/Y Next Wave, I had to decide something. There was an opportunity to take a week-long training course which was the first step towards becoming a qualified crew member. This training would include basic first aid, sea survival, firefighting, and social responsibility. It was called Standards of Training, Certification and Watchkeeping, or STCW for short because that's just too many words. It wasn't required but would be good for training purposes and just knowing more of what I was doing on a boat.

It was expensive though. Living on the financial giving of others, I never had much in my bank account, so I had to seriously consider my spending choices. The deal was that should I decide to take the course, the ministry would pay for it up front and I would pay it back in service to the ship over twenty-four months. The problem: I was only planning on spending six months on the boat. That meant I would have to pay back seventy-five percent of the cost of the course when I was done. This didn't make much sense. It didn't seem worth it to me.

So, I prayed about it.

I took the time to go down to the prayer room (well, boiler room turned prayer room) below the Chapel on The Oval to ask God if I should take the course.

I immediately heard an absolute yes.

I signed up the next day. It still didn't make sense, but I trusted in that yes more than my own understanding.

A month later, I was on a five-hour journey consisting of taxis, trains, tubes, coaches, ferries, and walking legs, which led to walking up the gangway to step foot on the deck that was to be my new home.

I was on a boat. Again. I could hardly believe it. I had just left what had been home for me surrounded by fields and walked onto what would become my home surrounded by water. I was in near disbelief that this was actually happening. I lugged my suitcase to my new cabin down the crew hallway and started unpacking. An idea five months in the making turned into my new and very real reality.

That was Sunday.

The next day, I began the STCW course. I had no idea what I was getting myself into as I woke up early on my first morning in my new home to make a packed lunch for myself before walking along the streets of Cowes to where I would be taking the course.

I walked in, took my seat, and was surrounded by a very diverse group of people. There were older men who needed more training to get more lucrative jobs, European ladies wanting to work on cruise ships as massage therapists, others interested in being more qualified to work towards being the skipper of their own yacht. Then there was me. A young, blonde-haired, blue-eyed girl from America volunteering to disciple others on a ship with a mission's organisation. Kind of the odd one out in that group.

Almost everyone was there in hopes of furthering their chances at finding a job. Some on pleasure yachts, some on cruise ships, some on fishing boats. When asked what I was doing, it was completely different than everyone else there. It just didn't make sense in the world's eyes. Sometimes mine as well. It still doesn't. I realised that I already had the job. My job was loving God and loving others, helping people be the best they could be through discipleship, working on the ship, living life to the fullest, serving in any way I could, being a blessing to others. Kind of an interesting job description but I was OK with it.

Day one was basic first aid. Always good knowledge to have. We had test dummies to practice performing CPR and learned a whole slew of other useful information. The next day was probably my favourite day – sea survival. We had to first put on dry suits (though mine didn't actually keep me too dry. Probably didn't have it on right.). We jumped into the sea to learn how to manoeuvre around in those uncomfortable suits, how to flip over a life raft and get into it, how to pull people from the water up into the life raft with you, and how to survive in that raft with the minimal supplies you had. It was a very exciting day.

The next two days were full of firefighting. We learned all about fire extinguishers, which ones to use on what kind of fire, how to put out fires using those extinguishers, hoses and fire blankets and how to use a breathing apparatus. After learning all these skills, we then put on the full firefighting equipment: jacket, trousers, boots, head cover, helmet and gloves, with the breathing apparatus strapped to our backs. We went in teams inside a fire-filled shipping container to put out a fire, find and rescue a planted fake casualty (or three), and get out safely with the whole team. It was incredibly dark and hot in that container, and we had to stay in line, feeling with our hands around the room to figure out where we were going. I got to be the one with the hose in front to put out the fire, and I found the little baby casualty we were to rescue (not a real baby). It was a lot of fun though I'm not sure I would want to do that again.

By the end of the week, I got my certificates, and it was official – I was considered a qualified crew member. How the heck was that a thing?

That was Monday through Friday.

The next day, we held an open boat. This was when we opened the ship to the public and people could come get a free tour of the decks. This was an easy way of showing people what we actually did and a little of what it was like on a boat. There were so many who came for that afternoon. I got to give my first tour of the ship even though I had only been there for a week. I had no idea what I was doing seventy-five percent of the time, and I definitely tried to hide in the galley with the candy and other baked goods to avoid giving another tour due to my lack of confidence in knowing anything. But it was a good taste of what would soon become a highlight.

That was Saturday.

I woke up Sunday morning to a fun surprise. I discovered we were no longer connected to the dock. We were out at sea, and we were moving. We were at anchor and my name was on the whiteboard to do an anchor watch. Umm, help? Having never even heard of an anchor watch, I knew this was going to make for an interesting day. What a great way to wake up. The wind and rain had come in hard, so it was decided in the middle of the night to let the mooring lines go that held us in place and head somewhere else to get away from the dock so as to not destroy the ship or the dock. I somehow completely missed the engines turning on in the middle of the night. I guess I was tired from quite a busy week.

I experienced my first anchor watch that afternoon. My job for an hour and a half was to sit in the wheelhouse watching the navigation system and radar to make sure we stayed within a certain radius. We moved around quite a bit, lots of figure eights through the water. The wind and rain and current of the water were rather strong, so the ship was rocking in every direction. I definitely got my first little taste of seasickness. Not pleasant, but that was nothing compared to the kind of seasickness I would come to experience later.

After spending the day at anchor, we brought the ship back into another dock, as our previous one had gotten a bit damaged from the storm. As we were coming alongside, someone thought it would be a good idea to tell the new girl (i.e. me) to jump off the boat onto the dock as we approached to attach the mooring lines. Without thinking much about how ridiculous that may have sounded, I didn't hesitate. With the wind and pounding rain on me, I climbed down the ladder on the port side hanging down, hopped to the dock below a few feet down and away, and raced to grab the mooring lines in the exact order I was told to as Captain Herman pulled her in.

I freaking loved it.

No New Nuts

DATE: September 2012
LOCATION: Cowes, Isle of Wight, England
      50° 45' 33.5" N
      1° 17' 41.6" W

Apparently, I'm allergic to pistachios.

I found this out the hard way.

Several years prior, I had an allergic reaction to cashews that sent me to the hospital. Nothing too terrible but a bit of an uncomfortable scare. I've never been a nut fan anyway (except peanut butter), so it was a surprise when I was suddenly throwing up in a public restroom one night at a theatre. I have also been allergic to dairy my whole life. So, I knew what it felt like for my body to reject something I ate.

I'll tell you now, it's not a fun experience.

I had been on the ship with these new people for all of two weeks at this point. Two bites into a delicious pasta salad (minus the capers and olives sprinkled throughout because I strongly dislike those ...), I felt a little tickle in my throat. It was the warning sign I needed to stop eating and start drinking water to drown it out. That had always been my tactic when eating dairy, and that always worked for me, so I figured that was my end-all solution for allergic reactions.

That was incorrect.

That will always be incorrect when it comes to nut allergies.

Take my word for it. Water does nothing.

A gallon of water later, I still felt horrible, quietly anticipating the possibility of something coming up. I hadn't thrown up around any of these people yet, so my nerves got the better of me. (I'd get over that real soon though ...) I calmly dismissed myself from the table, not drawing attention to the fact that I was pretty confident I was in the beginning stages of a bad allergic reaction, grabbed the nearest bucket (which was surprisingly easy to find on the way back to my cabin) swallowed some Benadryl and went horizontal in my bunk feeling nauseous. I had only made this known to one or two people. Again, I had just met these folks and didn't really know what to do and was quite embarrassed.

An hour later, the gallon of water caught up with me. I hobbled out of bed to the crew toilet.

But then I caught sight of myself in the mirror.

I just stared in disbelief. My face was nearly unrecognisable. I was a puffy red mess. My eyes were swollen half-shut and they hurt; my cheeks were bright red and looked like I just got back from getting my wisdom teeth yanked out. The back of my neck felt like I had a pillow wrapped around it with all the swelling, and there was a rash developing on my arms.

Not good.

I stepped out of the bathroom and said to the first person I saw, 'Umm, I need to go to the hospital.'

We called 999 (emergency services in England). They asked me a lot of questions about how I was doing, especially in regard to my airways. Thankfully my breathing was OK at that point. It could have been much worse, and I'm grateful it wasn't. They said there was an ambulance on the way, and I had to somehow describe where we were. When you live on a ship, that can sometimes be a challenge, but especially because I was still getting to know the area where we were in the marina since it was different from the day before.

With the ambulance on its way, I went out to sit on the curb to wait with Captain Herman and his wife, Nelleke, who made sure everything was OK and that they could find us. As we were sitting there waiting, the swelling kept swelling, and the rash spread more around my arms and started on my legs. My calm demeanour changed into worry and slight panic.

We saw an ambulance with lights flashing zoom past us – pretty sure they were looking for me. They eventually spotted us as Herman flagged them down when they came back our direction. When they got there, two lovely lady doctors came to check on me. They had me climb into the ambulance and lie on the bed.

When I got comfortable, I mean, as comfortable as I could get with the reaction my body was having and my fear intensifying by the second, they asked me what was wrong and what kinds of reactions I was experiencing. I was rather shocked and a bit offended by their questioning as I thought there was no possible way they could think that was how my face actually looked. Clearly, I couldn't possibly be this puffy, red mess they saw before them. As she pointed out though, they had to ask since they don't know what people look like normally. Honestly, good point, but still, that kind of hurt.

Covered by one of those amazingly warm hospital blankets and with an IV in me, they proceeded to inject me with fluids and other substances of which I don't remember the name. But what I do remember was adrenaline. What an experience that was.

As she began to poke these things into my arm, I was laughing at the ridiculousness of the situation, probably more as a defence mechanism than anything else. Then, I began laughing harder and rather uncontrollably. My defences quickly crumbled. About a minute later, the laughter stopped and was replaced with tears of pain. I was restless, writhing, hurting and crying, begging the question of when it was going to be over.

I was terrified. Another minute later, I was somehow back to laughing hysterically.

I guess that's why they call it an adrenaline rush.

After all this excitement, it stopped. I could finally relax, feeling like everything was going to be OK. They put the oxygen mask on my face, and I breathed in the freshest air I have ever breathed, and I was calm. Though exhausted. The swelling went down, the rash subsided and my eyes stopped hurting and opened up again. They wanted to take me to the hospital just to be certain everything was OK, and I agreed. I liked these two ladies. They had just saved my life.

They opened the doors of the ambulance and I saw Herman with his phone pointed in my direction to take a picture of what was happening inside. He had been out there waiting for me the whole time, conjuring up worst-case scenarios and taking a video as if I were dying inside because that's just the funny person he was. Not my finest moment, but what a way to have a bonding experience with others, I guess.

The doctors drove me to the hospital where I stayed for about an hour or so. They put another blanket on me, so I was nice and warm and cosy. I was finally free to go, and I was given a week's worth of steroids to take to be sure it was all out of my system. As I left, I decided it would be a really great idea to take these two blankets I was wrapped in. They didn't say anything about it, so why not?

I made it back to the ship with my blankets and was out by the time my head hit the pillow.

Thus, created a rule in my life – Kellie doesn't try new nuts. I'm sticking with that.

Several weeks later, I walked into my cabin to find a picture of me from the ambulance on my pillow. A reminder of that crazy night and the friendships it created. Thanks, Herman.

Leaving Isle of Wight

DATE: October 2012
LOCATION: The Solent – Isle of Wight
    50° 45' 54.4" N
    1° 21' 12.0" W

It was a typical day in the south of England on the Isle of Wight. Cloudy, cold and slightly damp. We cast off the mooring lines and made our way towards the English Channel. We were headed towards an even smaller island south called Jersey, making a pit stop in Guernsey, which is just off the coast of France. This was to be my very first sail on Next Wave, and I wasn't really sure what to expect besides having no idea what I was doing.

I was sitting quietly next to Tamara on the bench in front of the wheelhouse. We were looking out into the ocean as we made our course towards the open sea in front of us.

I asked her, 'Umm, is it weird that this feels normal?'

She simply answered, 'No, it's not weird.'

Flipping heck, I was sitting on a big ship sailing in the middle of the sea off the south coast of England with a group of people from all over the world I hardly knew ... and it felt normal. It oddly felt normal that I was standing inside a wheelhouse, practicing my knots, raising, setting and lowering each of the five different sails and learning how to helm, learning how to plot our position on the navigational chart, how to read the GPS, radar and navigational computer, understanding what we were on the lookout for in front of us (lights, buoys, ships), how to make tea in the galley while you're moving, and, most importantly, how to throw up on the leeward side of the ship (away from the wind) to avoid the wind blowing it back all over myself.

How that all felt normal, I have no idea. Maybe that's just what happens when you are right where you're supposed to be.

―――――⋞⋞―――――

I should mention just a couple sailor terms before we get any farther and I lose you (though hopefully you've noticed the footnotes by now ...):

Port – The left side of a boat when looking forward. (I always remembered that by thinking that the word 'port' had the same number of letters as 'left'.)

Starboard – The right side of a boat when looking forward. (Similarly, the word 'starboard' clearly had more letters then left so I could rule that out which told me it was 'right'.)

Aft/Stern – The back end of a boat.

Bow – The front of a boat.

That's all for now. The rest you can learn as you go.

―――――⋞⋞―――――

One night, I learned how to pack a sail. It was still cloudy, cold and slightly damp but also dark. We had to take the jib[8] down and pack it up before we could change our course. I had no idea what I was doing, but Daniel was there to show me how.

When someone started lowering the sail, I stood behind it while out on the bowsprit[9] to start flaking it from side to side as it came down. When that process was finished, we tied a bowline[10] on the end of a rope and attached it to the very top grommet on the sail and wrapped the rope around and through to create a ratchet sort of motion that would tighten it. (Whoever thought of all these rope tricks was a freaking genius.) Then, we took the rope around the sail again and through at a point a little farther down to ratchet again. We repeated this same motion until we reached the end, and it looked like a beautifully packed sail. Nice and tight.

―――――↙――――――

Helming is my favourite. Like, absolute favourite. I can't say that enough, though I might say it too much. To helm is to steer the ship. You stand behind the wheel in the wheelhouse (or outside on the deck if it's nice enough) and try your best to stay on course while the wind and sails and tide and swell are pushing you in all sorts of directions

Tamara taught me to helm. She explained that helming was like driving a car without power steering. After turning the wheel of a car, when you want to straighten up after the turn, the wheel corrects itself and comes back to its original centred position for you. There's no power steering on a ship. You have to do that part manually.

---

8   One of the three sails at the front of the ship, or forward sails.
9   A long wooden beam with a net underneath that sticks out over the water in the front of the ship that the forward sails are attached to.
10 A type of knot to make a fixed loop at the end of the rope. Classic sailor knot

After some more explanation and my watching her intently, trying to understand how she was taking into consideration all the elements that affected the rudder angle and thus the helming process, it was my turn.

'What's your course?'

'235 degrees.'

'Course, 235 degrees.'

I took the helm for the first time in the English Channel.

It's rather invigorating to suddenly be controlling such a large (and expensive) vessel housing a group of people in the middle of the sea. No pressure.

Probably one of the most valuable lessons Tamara taught me about helming was that typically, a lazy helmsman was a good helmsman. The reason being that a ship doesn't always respond right away to a change in the rudder angle. Sometimes it takes a few seconds or a few minutes to notice any change in direction. It's always different. If I turned the wheel two times, and immediately nothing happened so I then turned it again another two times, at some point, the ship would react and start swinging way too far to the side I steered. But if I waited a bit at first to see what would happen, I wouldn't have to correct it so much and would stay on course significantly better.

Helming was always a kind of puzzle for me that needed to be figured out. The conditions of the sea were different every day. Sometimes it changed every hour. It was all dependent on our speed, our intended heading, the wind direction and force, and the swell in the water. Elements both above and below us all played a part. Every time I was handed a new course, I had to take a few minutes to see and understand how the ship would respond with each turn of the wheel.

The more I practiced and the more I took the time to understand how she moved, the better helmsman I became.

I'm always someone with an inherent need to do things right, to be good at everything, to not make mistakes, to be perfect. It was a rare thing to always perfectly stay on course. So, if helming taught me anything (besides just adding to my list of random things I enjoy doing), it's to give yourself grace in what you're doing, in what you're learning. It takes time to get things right and that's OK.

The Burger Incident

DATE: October 2012
LOCATION: English Channel
50° 7' 24.1" N
1° 59' 8.3" W

The galley was always an adventure. Especially if you used the toaster at the same time someone was vacuuming the floor of the saloon because it would blow the breaker then someone would have to go down to the electrical closet to restore power. We really had to coordinate our cooking and cleaning efforts.

Something I quickly learned to be a challenge while sailing was cooking in the galley. In my personal opinion, the galley was quite possibly the worst place to be on a boat during a sail (well maybe the engine room but I didn't spend that much time there). Especially a rough sail. Whether it was cooking, doing dishes, making toast or tea or simply just being in there, it's just the worst. Some days were better than others, but most of the time, when I stepped foot into that galley, my stomach did a lot of flipping around – sometimes a bit too much for comfort. It was often quite warm. And there were a lot of smells floating around – most of the time not very good ones (except for when someone decided to boil a pot of water with ginger and lemon; that was always a welcome aroma). The pots and pans would be banging around in a contest of who could be the most obnoxiously loud; the baking beans in the cupboard would be rolling around like they just didn't care; cutlery drawers were revolting, throwing out forks and knives everywhere. And sometimes the power would go out and you would have to chop your vegetables with a headlamp attached to your head so you could see. When attempting the simplest things like making a cup of tea, it was easy to miss the mug and pour boiling water everywhere else but the cup. Everything had to be latched, locked, and bungeed or else something would break.

It was on this sail to Jersey that I first learned about the challenges one faces when entering the galley.

We all took turns being on different watches throughout the day and night. You'd be on two watches a day, the same time AM and PM. The watch schedule was typically as follows:

        00:00 – 04:00 / 12:00 – 16:00
        04:00 – 08:00 / 16:00 – 20:00
        08:00 – 12:00 / 20:00 – 00:00

They each had their pros and cons and different duties to attend to. And everyone had their favourite.

Those of us on the 04:00 – 08:00 / 16:00 – 20:00 watch was in charge of cooking dinner for everyone. Meal planning for sails can prove to be quite a challenge and must be thought through well. I don't think this particular meal was thought through well enough. Burgers and fries. Fries were easy enough. We put them in the oven and just left them for a while. Burgers, on the other hand, were not so easy, especially when making the patties from scratch. We liked to eat good food on board, and homemade burger patties taste way better than frozen ones. Good food equals happier people. But sometimes convenience can be better.

On one end of the galley, I was attempting to stand in one place and chop tomatoes without them rolling off the cutting board and splattering on the floor or dropping the knife on my toe. On the other end was Tamara, trying to keep the frying pan in place while flipping burgers and making sure the pan with uncooked burgers and the pan with cooked burgers stayed on the counter while also keeping her own balance and not burning herself over the stove. Seriously, one needed at least five arms to take on that task.

It was quite the endeavour, and as I was trying incredibly hard to concentrate on those tomatoes, the noises of the pans clanging and Tamara exclaiming her troubles took over, and my stomach started to turn on me. I tried to hold it all together as long as possible, but the moment came when I could hold it no longer. I quickly told Tamara I had to leave her to get some fresh air outside. What an introduction to proper seasickness. The first time during my first anchor watch felt puny in comparison to this. I had eaten some vegetable crisps at the recommendation of someone else and that was mistake. (I still can't even just look at a bag of vegetable crisps without feeling queasy …)

I shot out of the galley, up the skinny staircase, and out the door. Not to worry, I threw up on the leeward side, though it was still a most unpleasant experience. I went back inside the wheelhouse and saw someone else go down to the gallows in my place to help Tamara finish preparing the meal. I didn't think I could make it down those steps again, so it was a relief to have a replacement. I felt like a failure of a dinner prep partner, but I wasn't about to put myself back in that galley. And I don't think anyone else would have wanted me to either.

I had thought the difficulties of this meal were behind me, but they only escalated. It was now time to try to eat. I am usually a fan of burgers. This day, however, I just couldn't find within me any desire to take a bite. I felt awful, and the thought of food in general made me more nauseous. Tamara was struggling as well. She was feeling just as ill by this situation, though her stamina to carry on her duty was far superior to mine. But we knew we had to eat something. If we didn't, there would be nothing in our stomachs to inevitably throw up later, and when there is nothing there, it is the worst feeling ever. Believe me, it's not pleasant. It happened once, and it was awful.

We were sitting on the makeshift bench in the wheelhouse watching the horizon with the darkness of night getting darker with burgers and fries on a plate in our laps, trying to hold ourselves upright from the movement. As I forced the first small bite and attempted to chew and swallow, the only way to get it down was to yell.

'THIS TASTES SOOOOO GOOD, DOESN'T IT??'

'THIS IS THE BEST BURGER I HAVE EVER HAD IN MY LIFE!'

Yes, Tamara and I were both yelling at ourselves, each other, and the burger so painstakingly prepared in order to consume it and not throw it back up. Somehow, through all that yelling, we managed to get our burgers down. The fries not so much, but I no longer cared at that point. There was at least something in my stomach, and that's all that mattered.

Through this, I came to learn that yelling was a surprisingly great defence to seasickness. Because being seasick sucks. But I guess yelling at it with a friend is better than yelling at it by yourself, right?

Into Jersey

DATE: October 2012
LOCATION: Jersey, Channel Islands
    49° 10' 45.2" N
    2° 06' 49.2" W

After a quick pitstop in Guernsey where Captain Herman and First Mate Sam decided to take a very cold dip into the sea after one of their marathon training runs, we continued on to Jersey. This would be my second mooring operation and would be a bit more challenging. But just as cool. We were to be moored beside a huge stone wall. When the tide was out, the top of our mast barely reached the top of the wall, and when the tide was in, we were parallel to the top of that same wall. That was about a ten-metre variance, and it happened twice a day. Those were definitely the most extreme tide changes I would ever experience.

Next to this stone wall, we were going to be stern to the quay[11]. Being 'stern to' meant the butt of the ship was going to be back against the dock. It was quite the manoeuvre to manage. I should mention it was raining, and hard, when we were out handling all the mooring lines and fenders for this operation. When our stern line reached the quay, we had to inch back to the dock just a bit more. But a bit more with that big boat was no easy feat. Nelleke and I both grabbed the stern line from the aft deck once it was attached to the quay and pulled with all our might. We pulled and pulled until the ship inched into position. We locked off, and our job was done as the rest of the

---
11 A long platform next to the water to tie the boat to, also referred to as the quayside. Pronounced like 'key'.

crew handled the other lines so we could be held in place. I was tired and wet but had a huge smile on my face sitting on deck once we were secure. And we felt pretty good about ourselves at that show of strength.

Our week in Jersey consisted of an intense training week known as Day Skipper. During this course, we learned nautical terminology, ropework, how to use the safety equipment on board, how to use navigational charts for position plotting, course calculations and safety, right of way rules, understanding tides, using other navigational equipment like the radar, GPS and the electronic chart, and what different lights on ships and buoys meant. That was all wrapped into one week, which resulted in a final exam we needed to pass if we wanted to get that certificate.

The saloon became an interactive classroom with a lot of time spent on the floor looking at navigational charts doing math and on deck practicing knots and going through flashcards of all the different navigational lights and their meanings. It was learning like my brain hadn't had to do since I was in high school. Morning and afternoon, every day for five days we did this. My brain hurt by the end of it.

On the final day, we had several hours to take our exam which would result in either a pass or fail. There was a question-and-answer portion as well as a chart portion where we were to do a lot of position plotting, course calculations, and all of the other things we had learned. We had to do this all by memory and without cheat sheets. It was a hard test, but I passed and was handed the certificate.

This week added to the intensity of all that I was learning living on a boat, but sometimes you just have to learn all the new things at once and jump into the story headfirst.

The majority of the first sail from the Isle of Wight to Jersey before all that Day Skipper training was realising that I had absolutely no idea what I was doing. It was all brand new. But there was no time to dwell on that. It really didn't matter. I had to accept it and just jump in. I had to get wet. I had to take risks. I had to try. I was very aware that I had a lot to learn and understand if I was going to be of any use. So, I was eager to be involved in every opportunity to helm, to raise a sail, to harness up and go out on the bowsprit to tie up the jib, to plot our position on the chart, even to cook dinner in the galley. I wanted to be a part of it all. I had incredible teachers around me who knew what they were doing that I could learn from, so I took full advantage of that, no matter how overwhelming it felt at times.

The thing about that ship was that everyone saw my good and bad sides real fast. I realised there was nowhere for me to hide. I couldn't hide behind anyone, I couldn't hide who I was anymore, couldn't hide my shortcomings and insecurities, and that terrified me. I had always gotten by with perpetually being the person in the background, but that was no longer an option on this boat. I was a part of a very small crew and community; I was in front of the room teaching and leading worship; I was learning to lead sailing operations. If I made a mistake, everyone would see, and I hated making mistakes and I hated people seeing that.

We are meant to live in the fullness of who we are, but to get there takes putting ourselves in circumstances that stretch us. My comfort bubble burst within the first few weeks on Next Wave. But that kind of burst is a pivotal part of our stories as we move forward in life.

Sail to Cardiff

DATE: October 2012
LOCATION: Celtic Sea
49° 41' 51.4" N
5° 38' 58.0" W

We had been in Jersey for just one week before it was time to set sail again. This time headed for Cardiff, Wales. I was once again on the 04:00 – 08:00 / 16:00 – 20:00 watch during this four-day sail. Like I've said, there were ups and downs to each of the different watches throughout the day. For this particular one, it really messed up my sleep schedule. But the biggest plus was that we got to watch the sun both rise and set every morning and every night.

    This sail boasts of the most amazing sunset I have ever seen. And I've seen a lot of them over the years, in a plethora of places and different landscapes, but this one still tops them all. It probably always will. We were all on deck watching the amazing colours that were changing all around us. Some people were out enjoying it on the tip of the bowsprit, some lying on deck looking straight up, some sitting on the bench in front of the wheelhouse. We were completely surrounded. It was beautiful no matter which way you looked. There was no land in sight. Just us and the sea, engulfed in the array of colours put on display for only us to see. It was one of those sunsets when it hits you how freaking incredible and beautiful life is. There I was, on a boat in the middle of the sea, with people who were already starting to feel like family, watching the sky being painted with the most vibrant colours of reds, yellows, oranges and blues.

I had a moment when I was in the wheelhouse sitting next to Tamara and I thought of how glad I was to be there, to be fully present, to be part of what was happening right in front of me. I thought of the craziness of God's creativity in bringing me to a place such as this, doing the things I was doing. It had been hard in so many ways (like most new things in life), but it was moments like that which made it all worth it. Moments of sitting next to your friend, watching the sunset as you chase the horizon with the sounds of the sea blowing through your ears. It's important to stop every once in a while, to take in where you are, what you're doing, and who you're doing it with.

Not only was this a beautiful sail with perfect weather, but we also had a bit of a project that needed to be done before we could head into Cardiff. When we arrived, we were going to have to go through a lock to get to where we would be moored. But this particular lock would be tricky, not only because it was not very wide but with our bowsprit out in front of us, the ship was too long to fit for the lock door to close behind us. The only way we would be able to fit was to raise the bowsprit which would decrease our overall length by several metres.

I'm still not entirely sure why, but I was somehow the one given the responsibility of going out to the very tip of the bowsprit with a shackle I was, under no circumstances, allowed to drop in the water. Cool. I had to remove one piece of equipment and replace it with this little shackle smaller than the palm of my hand. While the task itself was simple enough, it was not the smoothest of waters and the wind was picking up a bit. I carefully hopped up onto the foredeck, attached myself to the safety line, and climbed along the net out to the very tip of the bowsprit, as far forward as I could go. I glanced down for a moment to the water far beneath my feet through the square gaps of the net, but that wasn't a great idea. I then looked forward to focus on my task. Through shaky hands, I unscrewed one bolt, put it in one jacket pocket, unzipped the other pocket, and took out the shackle. I was terrified I would drop one piece or the other of this small, two-piece shackle through my shaky hands, but to my relief, I got the job done successfully and made my way back on deck.

We then rigged a halyard[12] through that shackle I triumphantly exchanged which allowed us to raise the bowsprit. We fit ever so snug into that lock and sailed into Cardiff.

---

12 A rope used for raising and lowering the sails.

Sail to Glasgow

DATE: October 2012
LOCATION: River Clyde
55° 56' 18.9" N
4° 37' 01.1" W

I had just gotten some new thermal leggings and neon green waterproof trousers. I wanted to be warm and stay dry after two very cold and wet sails. Sometimes, getting ready for that warm and dry state was harder than it should have been. I was sitting on the floor of my tiny cabin trying to put on my leggings because sitting was often easier than standing when having to do certain things on a rocking ship. Reaching for my neon trousers while also searching under my bunk for my boots, we hit a wave, and suddenly, I found myself up close and personal with the door on the opposite side of the cabin as my slippery leggings slid me across the floor.

The ship rocked the other way, and I was back to where I began. After a moment's laugh at what just happened, I put one leg in, then the other into my trousers, a material much less likely to make me slip. On went the boots, and I finally stood to my feet, took a second to find my balance, grabbed my jacket hanging on the hook behind the door, and made my way up to the wheelhouse for watch.

The way from Cardiff to Glasgow led us up the River Clyde. It was a beautiful morning, so we were standing on deck gazing around at the beautiful land surrounding us close on either side. It was a pretty narrow channel with some amazing sights. There were fields upon fields and green trees and pathways and old buildings built on rock formations and dogs running around in freedom on the shore. And it was quiet. It was also wintertime in Scotland, which meant rather frigid temperatures. So, what do I do to stay warm when it's cold out? Exercise, of course. I had recently acquired an agility ladder from one of my favourite people back in Harpenden, so I brought it out and started doing circuits on deck. Thankfully, at least a couple people joined me, so I wasn't the only ridiculous one running around on deck trying to keep warm.

Wanting another vantage point to enjoy the view, I decided to climb up to the crow's nest on top of the forward mast. I took my time climbing up the ratlines to the top and hoisted myself up on the platform. It was quite the experience to be climbing up something while simultaneously moving forward through the water. I had only been up there before when we were still, so this was new.

After a few minutes of surveying the land on all sides of me, I looked down and saw Thomas, fellow crew member and bosun[13] at the time, rally a few people together. What was going on quickly became clear as suddenly, everyone was lined up on the rails on the starboard side.

Thomas shouted, 'One! Two! Three! Go!'

Then everyone ran.

Lined up against the port side now, Thomas yelled, 'Aaaaaand go!'

Back to starboard, 'Go!' Back to port, 'Go!'

They were rocking the boat.

The more it rocked, the more people came up from below deck to see what the heck was going on. Suddenly their smooth

---

13 Essentially a crew member responsible for maintenance of the ship and its equipment. Thomas did a lot of things.

sailing turned into a steady back and forth roll. Seeing what was happening, they joined the fun.

Watching and feeling this from the crow's nest was quite comical. It's a funny sight to see people running back and forth in unison on deck from such a height. I looked up to the aft mast and saw just how effective their efforts of rocking the boat were. It made my stomach a little queasy, but I was smiling too much to care.

Stuck in Glasgow

DATE: October 2012
LOCATION: Glasgow, Scotland
 55° 51' 52.9" N
 4° 18' 19.2" W

Things settled down on deck as we got closer to the Riverside Museum near where we were to be moored alongside. I was in the wheelhouse to escape the cold when I was suddenly overwhelmed by anxiety. I had no idea where it came from, what triggered it or say what I was so anxious about. But I just had a bad feeling as we pulled up alongside.

The reason became clear quickly upon arrival. Port officials had some questions about our registration. We had done everything right but apparently didn't tick some of their boxes. Next Wave didn't really fit into just one type of vessel classification so I think we just confused people. It was hard enough for me to understand it then let alone try to explain it now. What it resulted in was a word that still puts a bad taste in my mouth.

Detained.

Until we could prove we met their requirements and could tick all their boxes, we weren't allowed to move. We had only planned to be in Glasgow for one week but that plan suddenly became irritatingly open-ended.

Being stuck sucks.

That being stuck, that questioning of the ship's identity, made me start to question a whole lot of things myself. Who am I? Why am I here? What the heck am I doing? Why am I living on a freaking boat? What's my purpose? I felt insignificant. It suddenly felt like God didn't care and that he wasn't someone to keep His promises.

I think we all go through moments like that on a pretty regular basis. But it's these moments of questioning that are actually really good for us as much as they suck. If I didn't really know why I was doing what I was doing, what would be the point of doing it? If I didn't question whether God kept His promises, I would miss out on what comes when he proves me wrong and shows how incredibly he does keep those promises. If I didn't question whether or not he cared, I would miss out on realising how trustworthy he is.

I just wasn't there yet.

Because being stuck sucks, and that's all I could see.

Dinghy Training

DATE: November 2012
LOCATION: Glasgow, Scotland
   55° 51' 52.9" N
   4° 18' 19.2" W

There were a great many benefits to being crew on S/Y Next Wave. One such benefit was needing to know how to drive the dinghy. This was important for many reasons: In case we needed to rescue someone in the water, we would drop the dinghy, detach and motor out to them for a rescue. If we were at anchor, we would need to shuttle people back and forth from the ship to the shore. It could also be used as a grocery vessel or be used as an excuse to go out and take beautiful pictures of the ship with sails up at sea. Clearly, it was very important that I learn that valuable and necessary skill. So, one day during maintenance, Tamara decided it would be the perfect opportunity to teach me that skill. I whole-heartedly agreed.

 She took her seat at the back next to the outboard motor and showed me what was required when first getting into the dinghy, what equipment we needed to have with us for safety including the painter (a line that could be used to tie up the dinghy). She showed me how to turn the motor on, and as we steered away from the ship into the not so busy channel of the River Clyde, she was explaining along the way how to steer left and right, how to rev the engine for more speed and how to keep control of it. Then it was my turn.

 With the engine off, we swapped seats and I pulled hard on the cable to turn it back on. Next, I had to figure out how to move the throttle to go forward and steer simultaneously. It took a bit of focus to remember which setting moved us forward, how to go back, what was neutral and which way I had to turn the motor to steer left or right (which was intuitively backwards). We went up and down the channel for a while making a few turns and circles and figure eights to help me get used to steering.

Next was learning how to come alongside. This was an important process as you don't just want to ram into the side of the ship or the quayside. You gotta be gentle sometimes. Tamara demonstrated first. She aimed pretty much straight at where she wanted to end up and was pushing the gas just a bit to get some forward momentum. Then, when she got a certain distance away, she turned the rudder hard all the way to one side and quickly put it into neutral. This action resulted in perfectly gliding sideways right to where she wanted to be with a little bump on the quayside.

I had to follow that act.

Along the quayside were a few tyres hanging down acting as fenders. My goal was to aim at getting the dinghy right in the middle of two of those tyres. So that's what I attempted. I revved forward, put it in neutral and turned hard. I didn't quite get between my targets, but I also didn't ram into anything, so overall a good first try. I tried it a few more times to get practice and get a feel for how the dinghy responded to its rudder movement, a bit like the helming process.

I had one more go at getting between those tyres before the scheduled maintenance time was finished. One more chance at perfection. With stern concentration on my face, I lined up the front of the dinghy, revved forward, switched to neutral and turned hard. To my surprise and relief, we gracefully moved across the water directly in the middle of the two tyres I had been staring at. We grabbed hold of the dock and looked at each other in surprise and delight.

Wow. That was actually really good!

Running Through Puddles

DATE: November 2012
LOCATION: Kelvingrove Park, Glasgow, Scotland
55° 52' 9.1" N
4° 16' 51.7" W

One good thing about Glasgow was Kelvingrove Park. It was beautiful and massive and it was just the best. It was also the place I was first introduced to what would become my favourite tea - Peppermint Licorice. Tamara and I went for a walk through this park with a thermos full of this goodness. It has been steeping for a while and Tamara assured me that the longer it steeped, the better it became. She was right. It tasted so good from the very first sip and the lingering sweet aftertaste of the licorice root. The only thing was that towards the bottom of the thermos, we realised one of the tea bags had broken open which was unfortunate. But from that moment, I always went for the peppermint licorice tea.

Throughout the previous two years, running had kind of become my thing. Not only was it some much-needed exercise, but it was my way of relieving stress, processing things, and frankly, getting away from people. Being my very introverted self, constantly being surrounded by people in very tight spaces was a challenge. One I really had to learn how to manage. Like I said before, I couldn't hide anymore, and I kind of hated that.

I wasn't running for distance then. I wasn't running for speed or even consistency. I was running to find balance with my emotions. I hated being stuck. I hated the constant change in our schedule and not knowing when we could leave Glasgow. I was stressed, frustrated and cold.

The best time for me to run with our daily schedule was at 07:00, just before breakfast. It was wintertime in Scotland, so mornings were cold. This was a different kind of cold though, very different from the Colorado winters I'd grown up in and loved. Colorado is a dry cold. Scotland is very wet. That kind of cold gets in your bones and stays there. Not only was the air wet with humidity, but it was also wet with rain. Rain meant drenched runs. But rain also meant puddles.

I quickly discovered these puddles of various sizes along the side of the road and the pathways winding throughout Kelvingrove Park. I was usually apt to avoid them because wet socks are the worst. But there was one dreary morning when I couldn't deny the sudden urge to jump hard into a massive puddle and splash up as much water as I possibly could. At this point, I was already soaked through from the rain, so what was a little extra splash?

I saw my target and ran with a determination that was ever so satisfied as I leapt into the air. I was instantly surrounded by a wall in all directions as my feet hit the pavement below inches of ice-cold water. As the water settled around me, a massive smile came across my face standing in the middle of a puddle. I hadn't experienced that kind of joy for a while. And it was about damn time.

Breakfast time was approaching, and I knew I had to get back before it was cleaned up and I missed my chance at warming up with a bowl of hot oats and cup of warm tea. I started racing back to the ship with more energy than I had begun with. I would pass smaller puddles and do a quick bound in and out of them along the path back home. Each one drenching me more with water and with joy.

Rejoice in the Lord always.
I will say it again: Rejoice!
Philippians 4:4

There is always something to rejoice in. It doesn't matter your circumstances or what you're going through. There is *always* a reason to rejoice. But you have to choose it. And sometimes you have to do something that forces you to choose it.

Like jumping through icy puddles during winter in Scotland.

No Longer Detained

DATE: *December 2012*
LOCATION: *Irish Sea*
54° 23' 48.4" N
4° 57' 26.7" W

What should have only been one week turned into one month of being detained in Glasgow. Our maintenance requirements increased tremendously with every inspection. We did drill after drill to be sure we as crew knew how to handle any and every kind of emergency situation. We had one final inspection to prove it.

After performing every step in each of our positions to the best of our abilities, going as far as actually turning the fire hose on in one of the cabins to put out a 'fire' during a drill, we anxiously awaited their decision.

Pass.

It was like a breath of fresh air in our lungs. Like a heavy weight being thrown to the ground, and we could walk a little lighter. Relief set in. That anxiety I had felt when we arrived finally faded. We weren't stuck anymore. We could go.

But with conditions.

We would only be allowed to sail with qualified crew members and no additional passengers. This meant that three-quarters of our community were not allowed to sail with us. This left only eight crew members to sail the 220 nautical miles south to Liverpool. The rest had to stay in a hostel and catch a coach to meet us there two days later.

Going from a community of twenty-four to a crew of eight meant longer watches more frequently. Instead of being on watch four hours, then off for eight, we were on a schedule of six hours on, six hours off. That left very little rest time for any of us. We managed these watches with only four people on each and shared all cooking and cleaning duties.

The first morning, I took a little time to make myself breakfast in the galley. But remember how I've said that the galley was quite possibly the worst place to be on a sail? Well, I started to experience those familiar and uncomfortable feelings, so I opened the porthole to get a little fresh air blowing through to ease the stuffiness. It was effective enough to finish cooking, and then I went back up on watch.

About an hour later, the swell started to pick up, so the ship was rocking back and forth and insinuating a war in the galley between the pots and pans. We always tried to secure things as best we could so they wouldn't fall out of their places, but they still sometimes had some room in their places to move around and make a raucous. At one point, I went down there just to check that everything was OK and nothing was shattered like it sounded. Right as I stepped into the galley, the boat heeled over on the starboard side, pushing me in forward, and I immediately looked up at the open porthole in front of me while bracing myself in the doorway just as a wave crashed up and poured in through the small opening. Crap. I used all my strength and core balance to climb up on the soaked counter (little legs always made reaching things hard) to close the porthole just before another wave hit and before that wave might knock me backwards off the counter. I landed on my feet to a galley full of water. There was a metal bar on the bottom of the doorway so the water didn't spill out into the hallway, but that meant it was sloshing all throughout the galley floor.

First Mate Sam came down to check on what had happened after my exclamations at being soaked with seawater. Seeing the aftermath, he just smirked at me without a word and went to go grab the mop. We mopped up the water through little chuckles at what just happened.

Open portholes are great, but they are also dangerous if forgotten about. Remember that for later.

I wanted to take advantage of not having very many people to fight for the washing machine, so I decided to clean some clothes. However, our washing machine was not a fan of sailing, and when it was rocking back and forth, it tended to not work well, if at all. Not only that, but we also had some power issues which weren't really resolved. I started a load and an hour later, towards the end of my watch at around midnight, came back to put it in the dryer but found my clothes in a puddle of soapy water. My plan had been to quickly throw my clothes in the dryer so I could try to get as much sleep as I could before my next watch only six hours later. Then, I'd wake up with clean, dry clothes. That, unfortunately, was not how it worked out. A trend of plans not working out was formulating, and I didn't like that. I tried my best to rinse and wring them out into the shower (with the ship rocking back and forth, mind you) and get them in the dryer so they wouldn't just sit in that soapy water the whole time.

Well, the dryer decided it didn't want to start. Flipping heck. I had to do something to avoid ruining all the clothes I owned, so I resorted to grabbing a laundry line, some pegs and went down to an empty cabin below to string up the line and hang my clothes there for the night. Again, the ship was in full motion at this point, so that was much easier said than done. By the time I had everything hung up on the line, it was well past one in the morning, and I had to be up by 05:45 at the very latest to get ready for my next watch. Frustrated at the thought of only getting maybe four hours of sleep, I went back to my cabin, wrapped my entire arm around my mattress to keep me in place on my bed and tried as hard as I could to get to sleep fast.

A few short hours of sleep later, I went to check on my clothes, and lo and behold, they were still incredibly wet. Those cabins didn't always have the best ventilation, especially when needing good airflow to dry sopping wet clothes. I just gave up for the day, left them hanging, and went back on watch, deciding to deal with it when we finally got into Liverpool. I pretty much wore the same clothes every day anyways so nobody noticed or cared.

A little over halfway through this sail, we were all incredibly tired. Everyone had been working so hard to keep the ship going with a tough watch schedule, so we decided to take a break. We slowed down, lowered the anchor, and took a moment to stop and have lunch. Happy with that decision, I grabbed my plate of food and headed up to the main deck, taking a seat on the bench in front of the wheelhouse while everyone else stayed down in the saloon to eat. I needed a quiet moment.

Between bites, I looked out at the horizon, watched the sea on all sides and could just breathe. Tamara came up a few minutes into my quiet moment. We looked at each other, and she sat down next to me. Between bites, we would look out at the horizon, enjoying the view, the fresh air, the sunshine and each other's company. Not a word was spoken between us. We didn't need words. We understood each other's silence and allowed it to refresh us both.

Coming into Liverpool

DATE: December 2012
LOCATION: Liverpool, England
      53° 24' 5.9" N
      2° 59' 32.4" W

It was the third of December, and we were sailing through the Irish Sea, getting closer to Liverpool. Nearing the entrance of the River Mersey, red and green buoys, or channel markers, directed the way in. I was tasked with piloting[14] into the River Mersey and into Canning Dock to be moored right next to Royal Albert Dock in the heart of Liverpool. I was almost back to the same spot where this crazy journey had begun.

    Helming had quickly become my absolute favourite part of sailing during the three sails I had been on if I hadn't already mentioned that. When the course would be passed on to me, I would usually keep a close, constant watch on the compass to stay headed in the right direction and on our intended course.

    This time was different.

    Using each buoy ahead as a reference point, I kept our bow within the channel lines. Most of the time, I would claim perfection on this pilotage, but other times, I would get a little nod from the captain telling me I should probably steer a bit farther away from them to avoid collision with a buoy. He was probably right. There might have been a couple close calls no one else knew about with those channel markers.

---

14 To direct a ship through an area of water or into port (also pilot or pilotage).

Watching the Liverpool skyline come closer into view as the sun was rising in the early hours of the day, I couldn't believe my life. Exactly one year ago to that day, I had taken a one-way flight back to England with open hands and a very vague idea of what the next year might look like. Four months later, I got off a bus in Liverpool with open hands to an opportunity I didn't see coming. Five months after that, I disembarked a ferry on the Isle of Wight with open hands to unknown adventures to come from living on a sailboat.

Every step was an invitation to something new. An invitation I eagerly kept saying yes to.

While piloting between those buoys, I thought back to all that year had brought. How I walked with open hands to God, and he filled them to overflowing. How I cultivated amazing friendships with some amazing people. How I learned how to helm, how to pump out the greywater, how to drive a dinghy, how to throw up on the leeward side, how to coil a rope, how to suit up for fire drills, how to raise and lower the sails and tie them up correctly. How I got to travel to all these amazing new places on the coolest mode of transportation.

It was a pretty sweet year.

———— ⟨ ⟵ ————

As we found ourselves in the heart of the River Mersey, we made our way to the entrance to Canning Dock. Because of the height of tide throughout the day, this entrance was only able to open for a short window of time during certain hours of the day. It was a lock (similar to Cardiff) to keep the height of water the same inside the dock while the actual tide constantly changed quite drastically outside it.

While we were waiting, with the help of the captain's orders, I moved the rudder around using the fancy electric steering that I had never used before. There were two buttons, red for port and green for starboard, and they moved the rudder just like the wheel but a whole lot faster (and a lot louder). Definitely not as fun but effective when needing to do quick manoeuvres. I had to help keep the ship steady in the windy river, and when the lock opened, I followed the captain's orders and steered us into the dock.

On a calm day, steering into Canning Dock would be a challenge. It was a small entrance that was barely wider than Next Wave was wide. So, add in some windy conditions, and you're in for a momentary adventure. We were coming in faster than we probably should have and didn't quite make the turn sharp enough. The tip of our port bow rammed into the side of the lock despite best efforts to throw a fender down there to try to soften the blow. Oops. It was a bit of a shake to the ship, but with Next Wave's hull being made of steel, I'm pretty sure we did more damage to the wall than the wall did to us.

After that unfortunate incident, we slowly made our way to our spot, the same spot where I first crossed over the gangway, at the entrance to Albert Dock, just in front of the Pumphouse pub.

We were home.

Our Stories

DATE: December 2012
LOCATION: Liverpool, England
53° 24' 5.9" N
2° 59' 32.4" W

I love stories.

I love that life is simply that – a story. I love that life consists of stories within a story – and stories within a story within a story. I love that one story in your life shapes the next. I love that one story in your life always relates to a bigger part of your greater story and someone else's story.

We held an Open Boat on Next Wave once a week in Liverpool. By this point, I knew my way around a whole lot better than that first time so I wasn't hiding in the galley anymore. I loved getting to open our doors and invite people onto the ship to give them a tour, tell them about who we were and what we did and have a conversation over tea and biscuits.

One Saturday, a man came on board and was pretty quiet during the whole tour. He had come with a friend who was far more outgoing than he was, so he just quietly walked behind her the whole time. He didn't say a word. When the tour ended back in the saloon full of people, I grabbed a cup of tea for them and sat down at a table. With a cup of tea in his hand, he suddenly started telling me his life story. Tea just has that effect on people, I guess. With that first sip, sometimes your concerns and insecurities melt away. I could immediately see that God was trying to get a hold of him and change his life. It was apparent even in the story of how he happened to board our boat by chance that afternoon. We had a great conversation together, and at the end I prayed for him.

He asked, 'Am I supposed to feel different? Because something feels different.'

'That's pretty normal. That's what happens when you take a step closer to God.'

I got to be part of his story that day. And he is now part of mine.

I think God puts the right people in our lives exactly when you need them. Some for a long time, others for just a short time. But the amount of time doesn't matter. What matters is what you do with that time you're given with them and seeing their impact. I started recognizing the story I was living and who was a part of my story and who's story I was a part of.

It's our stories that shape us.

It's our stories that inspire others, that encourage others, that bring life to others, that allow us to relate to others. It is hearing others' stories that we are inspired, that we are encouraged, that we come to life, that we relate to them. But that only happens when we don't keep our story locked within ourselves.

Do something new. Do what makes you come alive. It is when you come alive, when you truly live, that the best stories are written. And it will be a story that brings life to anyone who reads it, anyone who sees it lived.

We all have a story worth telling.

To Something New

What if the point of where God has you is to do something that is beyond you?

Pastor Nathan once said that in a sermon. I listened to it months after he actually gave it while sitting at a grocery store in Gibraltar (we'll get there) because that was the best place I could go to get decent internet. I wrote that line on a piece of paper and taped it to the walls of my bunk to remind myself of that every day. To remind me that though very little made sense, God was doing something far greater in the midst of it.

I can sum up my first experiences on board S/Y Next Wave in one sentence: I had no idea what I was doing, but I just did it anyway. I had never lived on a boat. I had never tied a bowline before, never plotted a position, never raised and set a sail, never stood behind a helm.

This crazy adventure began because I said yes to an invitation to something new. And it was an invitation to begin letting God do something far beyond me. My eyes and hands were wide open with hope and anticipation at what could be in front of me. I had no idea what that was, but that didn't matter.

I jumped into the unknown, into the uncertainty, because someone invited me. First, because someone wanted to share how cool living on Next Wave was for them, and another someone who saw an opportunity for me to be challenged and to grow. God used those someones to get my attention. To get me to see that maybe God was inviting me to so much more than I could ask for or imagine, even if I had to start by having no idea what I was doing.

What if the point of where God has you is to do something that is beyond you?

Part 2
TO SEE AND KNOW

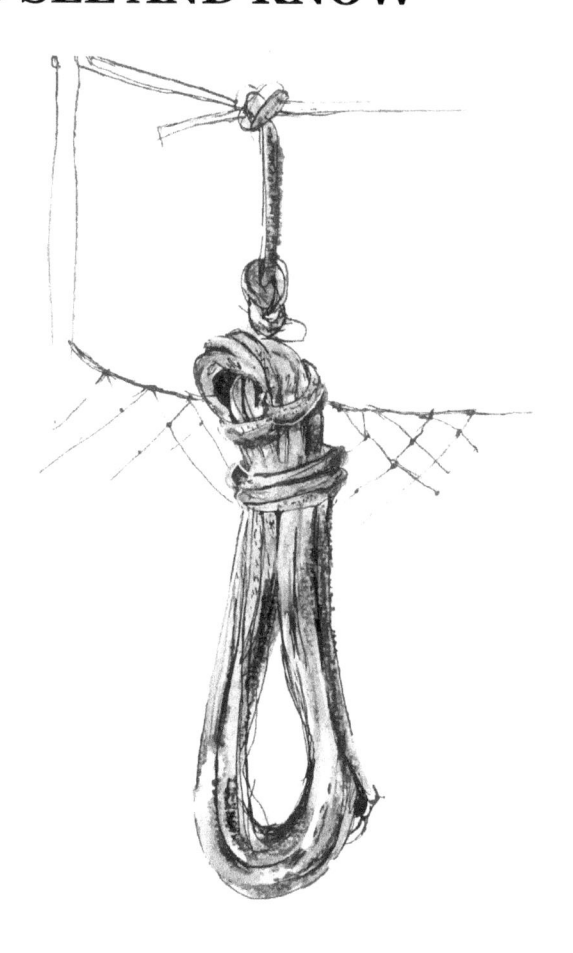

October 2013 – December 2013

Birkenhead, England – Falmouth, England: 2 days, 364 nm
Falmouth, England – Brest, France: 2 days, 227 nm
Brest, France – Viveiro, Spain: 3 days, 420 nm
Viveiro, Spain – Gibraltar: 4 days, 698 nm
Gibraltar – Gozo, Malta: 7 days, 1,036 nm

To See and Know

DATE: Summer 2013
LOCATION: Littleton, Colorado
    39° 34' 17.9" N
    105° 6' 12.9" W

'God created you for a special purpose, and until you walk through all the doors that he opens, you'll not figure out his plans for your life. Keep walking and believing, and you'll find your way.'

Dad

I spent the summer of 2013 at home in Colorado, taking a break to see family and friends after having been away for a long while. I needed to recharge, refocus and re-evaluate what I was doing with my life. Living on a boat kind of flipped my world upside down. The thing was, being home kind of made it hard for me to want to go back to Next Wave. But being home was also hard. So much had changed in and around me that home felt as much like home as Next Wave felt like home. And home also felt less like home as Next Wave felt less like home. I was torn between two wonderful and challenging lives. It was a weird thing.

My gut knew I had to go back though. I had made a two-year commitment, and I didn't want to back out of that. The loyalty part of me never wants to disappoint. Plus, I still felt like it was where God wanted me to be. So, I booked a one-way flight back to England for the end of the summer to re-join crew on Next Wave. With that decided, I felt this desire grow within me.

Something I wanted to commit to. One day, I spelled it out quite simply in my journal:

I want a faith that hopes and trusts to see and know God in everything.

I quickly came to realise that this seeing, this knowing, this trusting and hoping wouldn't always be pretty. It wouldn't always be these great epiphany moments when all was right within me and everything made sense. More often than not, it would be a painful process. I had struggled for a long time with trusting that where God was leading me was going to be good. So, when the storms hit, both inside and all around me, this journey of seeing and knowing God became a lot less appealing to be on.

But if I've learned anything from living on a boat, it's that the storms in the night make for the best sunrises in the morning.

God invites us to see and know him because he already sees and knows us. Because he already loves us. And because he knows that when we see and know him, we will get to live in the fullness of who he's created us to be because we will know the love he has for us. The kind of love that surpasses all understanding.

Thanks to an Irishman

DATE: September 2013
LOCATION: London, England
  51° 29' 39.6" N
  0° 8' 47.2" W

I woke up to a beautiful, cool, sunny morning on The Oval in Harpenden, England again after the long journey across the pond. The Oval was always the place I could come back to. The day began with a walk down Cooters End Lane, so I was off to a good start.

 I was headed north to Liverpool again to meet up with the ship. That journey would start with a walk to the Harpenden train station, then a train ride into London, a quick jaunt on the Underground, and another walk to Victoria Coach Station to catch a coach up to Liverpool. But it wouldn't end there because then I'd have to take another train in Liverpool across the river over to another town called Birkenhead which was where Next Wave was docked. I wasn't thrilled about that part but what was I to do?

 I was cutting it rather close on time to catch the coach, as well as lacking in strength from lugging around two heavy bags. I'm someone who always likes, well, needs, to be on time, so the thought of being late was starting to stress me out. I walked a bit faster than my normal quick pace. The thing with the Underground is it requires a lot of walking in between the trains, and there are stairs. Lots of stairs. And getting out at Victoria Station to get up to the street level included four flights of those stairs. Not ideal with a suitcase and guitar case in both hands.

To my surprise and relief, as I approached each flight of these stairs, there was always someone right behind me who decided to be a kind human and immediately grabbed the back of my suitcase to help me lift it up. Sometimes without my asking. I just had to glance back with a look on my face indicating that help would be appreciated (and clearly needed), and there was always someone who received the message.

I reached the street level and started what felt like the longest walk ever to the coach station, sweating by this point at how brisk my pace had to be to catch this bus. Weaving in and out of the crowded London streets was going to be a task with all my luggage. Turning the first corner though, an Irishman named Patrick stopped me and asked if I needed some help.

I quickly accepted his help, handed him my guitar case, and kept briskly walking.

We walked and talked as he carried my guitar for me, all the while my wondering how out of his way he was probably walking to help me. I told him about where I was going, and he seemed intrigued at the idea of living on a sailboat. He was a lovely gentleman, and I was incredibly grateful for his help. He carried my bag all the way into the coach station until I got to the door which led to my bus.

I thanked him profusely for helping and took back my guitar. Saying goodbye, he asked if I would say a prayer for him. I told him I absolutely would.

I was the last passenger to board the bus. They closed the doors right behind me. I made it just in time, and it was thanks to an Irishman that I did. I plopped down in my seat in utter exhaustion. When I composed myself a bit, it finally hit me that I was back in England. I was going back to Liverpool. I would soon be back on Next Wave. I felt real good about my decision.

Stuck in Birkenhead

DATE: September 2013
LOCATION: Birkenhead, England
53° 24' 33.27" N
3° 3' 9.0" W

Arriving back on board, we were docked in Birkenhead doing some necessary maintenance projects. The boat was in a re-fit season, meaning it was like walking onto a construction site. Except it was also my house so that was weird. I learned that I couldn't expect to slowly ease back into life on Next Wave but had to just jump back in real quick and get my hands dirty, oily even.

Birkenhead is a city just on the other side of the River Mersey from Liverpool. I had come to love Liverpool so much that to be looking at the city from a distance was rather disappointing. Birkenhead was not my favourite place, especially when being so close to my actual favourite place.

There were a few times I got to make a trip over to the city though. I'm pretty sure I came up with any excuse I could. Tamara and I spent one morning over there doing some shopping to restock our hospitality bench supplies. We probably could have gotten it all in Birkenhead, but why do that when Liverpool was just better?

When our shopping was done, we both looked at each other having the same thought. We didn't want to go back just yet, and there was nothing we needed to rush back for. We quickly agreed that it would be a great idea to head over to our favourite pub, The Baltic Fleet, for a pint before heading back. It was not hard to convince ourselves how great of an idea that was.

It wasn't until we walked through the doors to an empty pub that we realised the time. It was only noon. We were the only patrons, and the pub had just opened its doors for the day. Already committed, we grabbed our pints, (my pint of choice being one of their delicious still ciders on tap), took a seat and enjoyed being in one of my favourite places with one of my favourite people drinking one of my favourite drinks. This was also when another new rule in my life was created – if it's any time after the noon hour, it's acceptable to have a pint.

This re-fit season meant it was out with the old and in with the new. We weren't anticipating just how many old things were on their way out though. The original plan had been to replace both the generators and sewage treatment system, among a plethora of other smaller projects. I had missed the majority of the heavy lifting by the time I got there, and we were supposed to have set sail south for Falmouth the day after I arrived. But you'd think I'd have gotten used to it by this point that hardly anything went according to plan. We definitely didn't leave the day after I arrived.

I got to work, attempting to clean the grease-covered ship as we were to have a group of new DTS students arriving in a few days. We wanted to have as much ready for their arrival as possible despite lingering maintenance projects spread throughout the decks. As much as we tried to be prepared, there was no way we could prepare for what the coming weeks would surprise us with.

Every day for over a month, it was one thing after another. The main priorities were the engine maintenance, two new generators, and the sewage treatment system. Once those projects were finished though, the radar broke. That radar was vital to our operations, so it was imperative that we got a new one as soon as possible. While the new radar was being installed, the fire alarm system decided it was done too. While waiting for parts to arrive for the new system to be installed and tested, the fridge broke. Getting an industrial-sized fridge out of that tight galley and bringing down a new one was no easy task. It just barely fit through the multiple set of doors, halls, and stairways it had to go through.

With the new fridge in place, and the extremely loud fire alarms going on and off throughout multiple days of testing, work began on attempting to fix the dryer. That dryer would take a stupidly long time to dry any sized load, as I had the unfortunate luck of experiencing, and with twenty-five people on board, we had a laundry schedule that needed to be kept to. It just wasn't cutting it. During their attempt to make the dryer more efficient, the washing machine followed suit with all the other appliances and crapped out on us and also needed replacing. (It was agreed to that the dryer wasn't a priority since it still technically worked, so it may or may not have just gotten thrown overboard at another point later on ...)

To recap, this was the equipment that needed to be repaired and/or replaced: the engine, two generators, sewage treatment system, radar, fire alarm system, refrigerator, dryer, and washing machine. Then, there were the countless fire drills and safety training. Also flies. There were lots of flies. It was one thing after another after another that needed work. I know more things went wrong to add to that list, but I'm pretty sure I blocked it all out of my memory.

This went on for what felt like forever.

I absolutely hated it. I had never been so stressed.

These broken things delayed and significantly changed our plans repeatedly. The DTS schedule for guest speakers and sail dates had to be rewritten six times over the course of three weeks. We had also planned to be rigged with brand new sails in Falmouth which had to continually be pushed back.

There was even an issue with the ship's ballast. This is what helped stabilise the ship and keep it submerged correctly. There was too much water on one side of the ballast tank, so we had to find a way to tip the boat to move it to the other side to even it out. Easier said than done for a 200-tonne boat. One night, someone had the brilliant idea to rock the boat. We had done it before going up the River Clyde. We had everyone line up on deck and started running back and forth to rock it as much as we possibly could to tip it over enough to even out the ballast tanks. We even swung out the boom[15] completely to one side to add more weight that way. Not sure how successful it was, but it was for sure a good time whether it worked as well as we hoped or not. We got to play around with some of the lines so we turned it into a lesson of sorts. Maybe? Maybe it was more just for fun.

I began to learn the importance of choosing to find joy in the middle of difficult situations. It was something I had to learn over and over and over.

While dealing with these broken things, we also were waiting for paperwork to come through in regard to our registration. In addition to the paperwork, we had to have a survey done in order for us to leave. This included several different inspections and demonstrations that proved we could perform emergency procedures. It meant drill upon drill and making sure everything was up to their standards and regulations. We made sure everyone knew all of their positions and backup positions for every type of situation. This was the same thing we had to

---

15   A large beam/pole attached to the mast which is connected to the bottom of a sail.

do when we were stuck in Glasgow, so it was all too familiar a feeling. That was the first time I was at least a tiny bit grateful for having gone through the hell of being detained in Glasgow because I at least knew how to deal with the situation a little better. But not much.

Stressful and exhausting barely covers it. All the crew worked so hard to push through everything going on. They put in the necessary work at each unfortunate turn. And while it was incredibly stressful, the reality was that all the new equipment and safety drills were aiding in raising the standards on board. Standards for the crew and the ship itself. Those things needed to be updated, and it made living and sailing safer and more efficient. We had 2,745 nautical miles to cover in the coming months, and this re-fit made us far more prepared than we would have been had things gone according to our original plans.

But that doesn't mean that I had to like any of it.

Running at Sea Level

DATE: September 2013
LOCATION: Birkenhead Park, England
      53° 23' 40.3" N
      3° 2' 35.2" W

One day, I was journaling while sitting in the wheelhouse next to the radar (before it decided to break) and the helm (everything in me just wanting to go sailing) after having gone on a gorgeous run through one of the best parks I had ever been to (the only thing I liked about Birkenhead), with the sounds of weather reports and other communications periodically coming over the radio while looking out at the misty night (though sadly not much to look at …) with my favourite peppermint licorice tea in my awesome Colorado mug my friend gifted me and the sound of popcorn being popped downstairs in the galley.

Yes, I know that is one incredibly long sentence, but I was having a nice moment away from the construction zone down below. This was part of my learning to find things to take joy in every once in a while, through the stress and constant irritating changes.

It was this moment that I became fully convinced that if I could successfully make a bed on Next Wave, I could make a bed anywhere. (It all connects, I promise.)

You try making a bed with less than two feet of headspace to work with. And then do that on a top bunk when you have short legs. It's a challenge. One becomes a bit more flexible and able to fit into tight spaces more effectively while attempting to crawl into the bed to put on a fitted sheet and duvet and make it nice and neat as you crawl out. It takes some skill. A skill which I was well on my way to acquiring.

I thought to myself, *making any bed after this is going to be a piece of cake.*

Most of my summer days in 2013 consisted of hiking, running, and rollerblading, all at a reasonably high altitude. Denver's not called the Mile High City for nothing – the air is a bit thinner there. But after a few days of needing to stop and catch my breath before I got to the point of passing out while doing something active (like walking up stairs ...), I finally adjusted to the altitude, and I could run for a solid hour without sucking up all the air with pain in my lungs.

When I was back at sea level, I noticed a significant difference in my breathing during my run in that I could actually breathe very easily, even while running. Just before sitting in the wheelhouse to enjoy my peppermint licorice tea, I had gone on a run and that realisation became very apparent. It was the fastest I had been able to run from the start, and I just kept going. It felt good. Really good. I felt like I could run forever simply because I could breathe.

I realise that a big part of that probably had to do with the fact that I rollerbladed at least three times a week for three months because I had the time, so that definitely got me into better shape. Consistency is always key. But aside from that – and the point that I'm trying to make – is that I could breathe. I could run better than I could before.

Because I trained at high altitude.

Being back on Next Wave had its ups and downs. Particularly being stuck in Birkenhead was a down with delays, schedule changes, coming into a new role with new responsibilities and a new community, and everything in between. It was busy. But there was a difference that time.

I knew I could do it. Whatever task or responsibility was placed on me, I trusted in my abilities to accomplish those tasks.

That's a good feeling. The things that had been a challenge for me in the beginning, I could go about doing with confidence. I understood things more and had a better perspective. That's not to say there wouldn't be things I didn't know how to do and wouldn't present me with new challenges. But again, this time was different; my mindset was completely different.

And it's because I trained at high altitude. (I don't mean that literally anymore, of course. The boat was and always would be a sea level.) I had learned to make a bed well in tight spaces. In my first months on board, I went about many challenges barely able to breathe, barely able to fit, trying to keep up and do what I was supposed to do despite having no idea what I was doing and going through some rough weather. It was hard. It was new. I was tired. I didn't often have time to catch my breath then.

But this time around, I could breathe.

At first, I was a little worried about having that confidence. I thought it meant that I felt like I didn't need God to help me anymore and that he wasn't around as much because I was capable of doing it on my own. But that's not true. I felt his presence more on that first run back at sea level than I had in a long time. I knew he was with me in everything, and he had prepared and strengthened me (most times the hard way) for what he wanted me to do and who he wanted me to be and what was to come.

Maybe that's where that confidence came from in the first place.

Probably.

I think they call that growth.

It's the things that challenge your breathing and flexibility that prepares you most for what's coming on the horizon. And sometimes, you have to train at high altitude to run the next race to the best of your ability.

Status of the Heads

DATE: September 2013
LOCATION: Birkenhead, England
  53° 24' 33.2" N
  3° 3' 9.0" W

I believe that in every person's life, there are many moments of realising just how much you truly appreciate what you have. That appreciation tends to come when you suddenly don't have that thing anymore. It comes in all shapes and sizes and the level of appreciation often differs depending on the person and length of time that has been endured without that thing.

Living on a boat, one must give up many luxuries of life. Your personal space shrinks to a space smaller than a twin-size bed; your day off sometimes consists of rushing on deck during a sudden storm to batten down the hatches; and your quiet, lazy Saturday morning ritual is disrupted by at least ten people vying for the eggs in the cupboard you have to climb on the counter to reach. Or in our case on Next Wave, you never know what the status of the heads will be.

And by 'heads', I mean toilets.

Yes, I'm talking about toilets.

We followed the rule of 'If it's yellow, let it mellow. If it's brown, flush it down.' I have had to follow this rule plenty of times on youth trips in high school, but that was only for a few days out of the summer. On those trips, it didn't matter too much because, by the end of the couple days, you knew you were going home to your own personal toilet you could flush whenever you wanted. We didn't have that luxury on Next Wave. That rule was what we had to live with daily. One would often go to the toilet to discover some yellow substance and sometimes a little surprise waiting. And on a sail, while rocking back and forth, that was the last thing you wanted to see (or smell) when going to the head.

I know this sounds disgusting – most likely creating a rather unpleasant image in your mind and probably making you question the content of this particular chapter, and for that, I kind of apologise. These kinds of topics were a normal part of our everyday lives on the boat.

The reason I mention this is not just to give you a glimpse of the kinds of things one might deal with while living on a sailboat with a lot of people but to emphasise my deep appreciation when one day, the rules changed forever.

Mealtimes were the time to make community-wide announcements prompted by the ringing of a bell. At lunch, one of our engineers stood up, rang the bell and all went quiet. We were still very much stuck in Birkenhead with countless renovations happening throughout the ship; some we wished didn't have to happen, like testing the fire alarms over and over all day long. That gets old real quick. At this point, most of the announcements we heard during mealtimes were less than encouraging. It usually meant something else was changing in our ever-changing circumstances, that more delays or drills or maintenance would be imminent. I began to always anticipate the worst when that bell rang. My stress levels always went up at that sound. There weren't too many happy faces in the room as he began to speak.

But then …

He told us something we weren't expecting.

Something glorious.

We could flush the toilets.

Every. Time.

We no longer had to let it mellow.

After a few seconds of quiet disbelief, it hit us. We could flush every time now. We finally had the underappreciated luxury of properly flushing toilets back in our lives. All that effort put into the new sewage treatment system had finally paid off. It felt like the beginning of things finally coming together.

There was much rejoicing.

It wasn't long after this that we were finally able to sail out of Birkenhead and be on our way to Falmouth, England so we could be fitted with a couple brand new sails. All the hard work everyone had put in was being realized as we cast off the mooring lines to finally be on our way.

Again, there was much rejoicing.

Glowing Dolphins

DATE: October 2013
LOCATION: Sail – Birkenhead to Falmouth, England
      51° 19' 54.8" N
      5° 24' 23.2" W

It was 23:45, and I was on deck preparing myself for my next four-hour watch from midnight to 04:00. We were on a two-and-a-half-day sail to Falmouth, on the southwest tip of England. We had finally finished all the repairs and met the necessary requirements and were finally able to set sail which felt so good. I had my peppermint licorice tea in hand, leaning against the starboard rail, enjoying the fresh air and steady movement of the ship. Out of the darkness, I spotted this strange light out in the distance. Something was jumping and swimming through the water and coming towards us fast. I kept squinting into the distance, leaning farther out over the rail in attempts to make out what it was as it raced closer to us. Suddenly, I could see them.

They were dolphins.

And they were glowing.

The previous day, we had seen our fair share of dolphin pods in the water playing around. As we were gliding over the waters, they somehow found us and started playing and showing off in our wake on the port bow. They swam with us for hours and then would disappear. It's pretty incredible when you get to witness something like that up close.

So, these glowing dolphins in the night: It was so dark all around, and all I could see across the waters was the shape of a dolphin being lit up by what seemed like greenish-blue lights. Then more of them joined. A green stream followed each one as they sped through the water, surfing in our wake, disappearing for just a moment when they would jump out of the water into the dark night air. Then the light would reappear as they splashed back down. I could hardly believe what I was seeing.

I certainly don't know all the scientific reasons as to how this bioluminescence stuff works. I don't need to know. I'm just glad it's a thing that happens. Because it's quite beautiful. Especially in the middle of the night out at sea with no land in sight.

Leaning over the starboard bow with a line of others next to me, watching these glowing dolphins soar along with us through the water, I froze as I suddenly remembered something. Something significant. Something I had forgotten about for a year and a half.

One night during my first visit to the ship in Liverpool, someone had told a story about a time they were sailing and saw glowing dolphins in the water. They described it in great detail, and it sounded amazing. That was the same night God asked me to dream. So, the next morning, when I was at the café in Waterstones writing that dream list in my tie-dye tape-covered notebook, I thought back to that story I was so enthralled with.

I wrote on my list that I wanted to see glowing dolphins.

I wrote it quickly then moved on to the next thing, thinking very little of it. At that point, I had no inclination whatsoever that I was ever going to step foot on the boat again after that trip. It was something I wrote in a manner of, *Huh, that could be cool someday*, but never thinking or believing or even imagining it could ever happen. There was just no way. So, I didn't dwell on the idea.

That was the last time glowing dolphins ever crossed my mind. Until a year and a half later in the middle of the night while sailing to Falmouth, England. I had completely forgotten about that tiny, seemingly insignificant and impossible desire of my heart until the moment I was actually living it. Until the moment I realised that God was right there satisfying a desire in my heart. And it happened in a way in which it unmistakably could only have been him that made it happen. Only him who brought that moment together perfectly. There was no way I could have made that happen on my own, out of my own will, strength, planning or work. Not. A. Chance.

Here's what I think happened: I think when God asked me to dream and began to see what I was writing, he had a good little chuckle to himself. That he looked at this list, smiled and then started scheming. He started brainstorming all the possible ways he could make every one of those things happen, as outrageous as they might have been. I'd be curious to know what other potential schemes he might have come up with.

Somehow, this is what he came up with … 'OK, so Kellie is going to go visit this ship and then go grocery shopping, and she's going to get excited about the seemingly impossible possibility of coming back to the ship someday. Then, a few weeks later, someone's going to ask her if she wants to join the ship, she'll say yes, and then she'll be crew for a little while. She's going to learn all these cool things; it's going to be hard but also awesome. Then, she'll go home for the summer, decide she'll want to come back, but then get stuck in Birkenhead for a little while and get real frustrated. Then, they'll finally get to leave with shiny new things, and in the middle of the night, while they're on their way to Falmouth, I'll have a pod of dolphins swim up to their exact location in the middle of the Celtic Sea, and then I'll throw some of that really cool bioluminescence stuff in the water so the dolphins look like they're glowing. She'll be drinking her favourite tea in her favourite mug on deck at the exact right moment to see them coming her way.

'And I'll remind her that I didn't forget.'

To get there, God knew I would have to go through some storms. I would have to go through the crashing waves and winds of the sea. I would have to go through the stress and anxiety of being stuck somewhere, feeling inadequate and angry at what was and wasn't happening. It wasn't going to be easy or perfect or beautiful every day. It was going to involve a lot of seasickness. But he knew he could find a way – the perfect way, and more often than not, the hard way – of making that moment happen so that through every up and down, all I would be able to see was that it was absolutely him and only him who made it happen.

Looking at the context of when these glowing dolphins happened, we had been stuck in Birkenhead where literally anything and everything seemed to go wrong. We waited and worked and waited and worked until we were finally allowed to sail. We had hope and a plan that then changed over and over again, and we were discouraged over and over. What we were hoping for wasn't happening when hoped. But it was out of that waiting, out of that struggle, out of that unfulfilled longing that the desires of our hearts were satisfied.

There finally came that moment when we were cleared to sail. And we were able to sail with brand new equipment that worked. God knew we needed those things to break then to avoid breaking during a potentially dangerous situation later on. To have lost our radar in the middle of the storms we were to face would not have been good. God wanted us to have the best; he wanted us to be ready for the sails, storms and adventures ahead.

Sometimes, well, most times, the waiting sucks. Waiting for a job, waiting for a relationship, waiting for a cure, waiting for life to make sense, waiting to figure it all out, waiting for whatever it is that you're waiting for. But what's not yet will always be worth it.

Not only did this show me the truth of all those Bible verses that talk about how he will satisfy the desires of our hearts, but I also saw in it his goodness, his faithfulness. He heard me, he saw me, he knew me. He remembered what I wrote on a piece of paper. And he used a pod of glowing dolphins in the middle of the night to remind me of that.

God is good and faithful. He knows and remembers our dreams, our desires. Even the ones which seem like a passing, impossible thought. Even ones that are so random yet so specific. Even ones about glowing dolphins. And he loves to bring things together in ways we could have never imagined to remind us that he doesn't ever forget.

Tying the Sail

DATE: October 2013
LOCATION: Sail – Falmouth, England to Brest, France
 49° 15' 5.3" N
 4° 58' 48.6" W

While still in Birkenhead with our actual sail date finally coming closer and becoming more secure as projects were finishing and the frequency with which things were breaking was lessening (to our great relief), I was asked to start training to be a watch leader. Immediately, I felt inadequate but also knew it was something important to work towards.

Being a watch leader was exactly as it sounds. I was tasked with leading a watch while at sea. This entailed keeping the course, setting the sails as necessary, cleaning or cooking duties (depending on the time of day), delegating watchkeeping tasks and making sure the engineer of the watch did their hourly engine checks, among other things. And I had to be present and doing all the things despite how crappy I might feel. That first watch as watch leader, I threw up on the hour, every hour. By the third and fourth hours, there was nothing left in my stomach to throw up. This meant that my body was forced to dig deeper and all that came out was yellow bile, which is the absolute most unpleasant experience I've ever had. And I still had to keep watch after that.

Being watch leader also meant I needed to know my stuff. I had learned an incredible amount from my previous sails, but I knew I needed a refresher course before I would be able to take that kind of responsibility on. It was a challenge I had to take up if I was going to contribute as a competent crew member.

Part of this responsibility included knowing how to handle emergency situations of all kinds, changing course to avoid running into another boat and remembering everyone's tea order. All of equal importance. (That's why we had a 'How Do You Like It?' sheet up on the wall in the galley with how everyone on board took their tea and coffee. It was more a challenge to get the right mug to the right person.)

During one of my first couple watches on our way across the English Channel to France, a line attached to our jib had snapped loose, sending the sail into a frenzy in the wind. We were still getting used to the new rigging system. We had to go out to lower it and fast. I sprang into action, sending people to various stations to get the job done. Some were at the sheets[16] to rein it in, some at the halyard to bring it down. I quickly put my harness and life jacket on and ordered Ben to follow suit. We were to be going out on the bowsprit to tie up the jib.

With the ship rocking in the swell and wind, dark grey clouds surrounding us, Ben and I attached ourselves to the safety line on the bowsprit and carefully climbed out on the net to reach the sail. When we got there, I suddenly froze trying to remember how the heck to actually tie the sail.

While I was sitting there on the net, feeling seasick from the exponentially greater movement out on the bowsprit, wet with sea spray, looking at the flaked sail we just lowered with the coiled rope in my hand trying hard to remember how to even begin, I caught sight of Ben looking up at me worried followed closely by him hollering in the way that is so iconically Ben. (If you know, you know ...) He also didn't really know what to do and was feeling sick, stressed and worried about the current predicament we found ourselves in.

---

16 A line attached to the corner of the sail to control letting the sail in or out to fill it based on the wind and course direction.

So, there I was, trying hard to help keep Ben calm while struggling to will my stomach to settle, racking my brain to remember the procedure while outside on the bowsprit directly over the water – at times feet below and others what felt like inches and my feet might take a cold dip – in the middle of an impending storm. (The situations I used to so often find myself in are comical now to look back on.) I decided I just had to start and hope muscle memory would take over. Thankfully, it did. With every turn of the rope and ratchet to make it tight (like Daniel taught me), we got the sail tied up. It was time to get the heck off that thing.

With Ben's hollering finished and him on his way off the bowsprit, I looked up from my spot on the net to see Tamara come on deck and sit on the bench in front of the wheelhouse. The moment I saw her, I let out a huge sigh of relief. She was helping me train as a watch leader and was to be with me on the second part of each of my watches. When I saw her, I knew everything was going to be OK. I made my way up to the main deck and just sat beside her.

'How you doing?' she asked.

Sigh.

When we arrived in port, Tamara and I went out for a much-needed glass of wine.

Engine Checks

It's just after dinner, and the clean-up crew is gathering leftovers and dirty dishes from the saloon. The tables are cleared while others still chat about the week's events or discuss a really good book or try to decide what movie to watch later and whether to watch it on the screen in the saloon or, a little more epically, on the staysail[17] on deck. The music turns up in the galley, bass booming through the speakers, and the party begins. Stacks of plates, cups and cutlery splash in the sink for a good wash and rinse before being placed in the tray and put through the sanitiser. The digital countdown goes three, two, one, then beeps its final beep. The door opens and a cloud of steam rises. Moving to the tea-towel-covered counter, the plates, cups and cutlery are dried and put back in their proper places.

But I'm not on clean-up crew tonight. I'm on duty. Engineer on duty to be exact. Now I'm certainly no engineer, so don't let that title mislead you. That just means that for this day, and many others to follow, I get to spend a little time in the engine room making sure things are working as they should (like I know how all things in an engine room should be working ...). And by 'a little time', I mean maybe ten minutes, depending on how long the greywater takes to pump out, but I'll get to that.

Up the stairs from the galley party, is the wheelhouse where there is a clipboard with a detailed spreadsheet containing different abbreviations, numbers, lines and checkboxes. I grab the clipboard, making sure the attached string actually had a pen on the other end, and make my way back downstairs.

The first stop is my cabin, the first one on the right, to grab a headlamp to help see all the readings, and maybe decide if I

---
17   One of the forward sails

should wear proper shoes or not. I decide on a yes. Safety first. But more realistically, I'd rather not get oil all over my clean(ish) feet. Next is the crew toilet and other crew cabin to read some gauges which I have forgotten the names and purposes of. I know they're important or else they wouldn't be on the list.

In the tiny crew toilet which contains a shower, sink, toilet, washer, dryer, laundry basket, hot water heater, a little rubbish bin and small cleaning supply cupboard all in one very small space, there is a small, dark gauge hiding in the back of the cupboard that is difficult to see its markings and level drawn on with sharpie. I mark the numbers on my sheet and move on. Next, I hesitantly knock on the other crew cabin door (the one on the left which I had lived in previously) as I make my entrance into someone else's space to read the gauge hidden behind the door with jackets and hanging trousers to dry. Once that is done, it's down the hall then left to the small staircase leading down to the engine room on the right.

Depending on whether or not we are on shore power or using our own generators to generate necessary power for the ship, the noise in the engine room could be deafening. I grab the earmuffs to protect my eardrums, flip the dog latches, pull hard and enter the engine room. After learning and practicing the process, I finally have my routine down. First, I check the day tank for its fuel level, note it and push the button to fill it back up, then go around checking the oil levels of the two generators and main engine while the day tank fills.

Next comes the dreaded greywater pump. Dreaded because of the problems it had previously given us on several occasions and also because I'm slightly scared of it. It requires patience and doing the right steps with the right equipment and the right buttons in the right order so as not to make it explode (a legitimate fear I may or may not have ...). There are two pumps to choose from, both of which require opening and closing a couple valves. It's important to know which valve is for which pump, which ones to open and which to keep closed. Looking at the general area of the pumps, there are about seven or eight different valves to choose from, each connected to one or both pumps. I make my choice and fully open two valves, and a third one I turn for exactly three rotations as I was taught. Once the right valves are open comes the priming. This means stepping up and standing awkwardly over the pump to reach a button in the back and hold it down, counting to sixty, though sometimes I count to seventy-five just to be on the safe side. I'm still unaware of what holding that button down actually does, but I do it anyway, believing it has a real purpose.

If you thought the valves were the trickiest part, here comes more. With the push of a button next to the priming button, the machine awakens with a great roar, hence more use for the earmuffs. I was taught to hold onto the pipes, feeling the water temperature change as it rushes through, as well as listen closely to the specific sounds it makes as it goes through its cycle to pump out all the used water collected from the sinks and showers across the ship. When the pipes become cold, I know it's almost finished as that indicates cool seawater rushing through, meaning no more greywater was present. One last pop and click of the machine, and it was done. I push the red button to stop, and the noise level significantly diminishes. I close the valves I had opened and the hard part is over. Phew.

By this point, the day tank is full, and the numbers can be marked on my clipboard and on the sheet in the engine room to know how much fuel we had used up since the last engine check. Next, I go to the generator not currently in use and prepare to turn it on. We switched which generator we were using for power every day. With the newly upgraded generators, all is electronic, and so with the touch of a button, the engine rumbles to life. After another look around to see that things are as they should be (to my very limited knowledge), I step out of the engine room, close the latch, take off the earmuffs and enjoy the relief of silence.

The last step is to go into the skinny electrical closest next to the engine room, turn a few switches and press a few more buttons to switch the power from generator one to generator two. I was well acquainted with this little closet from all the times I had to reset the breakers. Still with a headlamp lit on my head to make sure I'm doing it right (and because the lights were going to turn off for a moment), I cut the power from generator one. All power on the ship goes off for just a second and there is a rush of eight bangs echoing down the halls as all the fire doors slam shut throughout the ship. I quickly flip another switch for generator two so that light and power can be restored. Then it's one last trip back into the engine room to turn off generator one to give it a break.

Everyone knows what happens when the lights suddenly go off and the familiar noises of magnets letting go and doors slamming shut echo. This is just a part of everyday life on board. It's time to reset. Everyone helps push all the doors back open when the lights come back on. After one more sweep of the ship to reset the whole fire alarm system using seven different buttons scattered in random places on board (one being a small cupboard in the forward hallway next to one of Thomas's famous bean drawings), my work is done.

I make my way back up one then two flights of skinny steep stairs to the wheelhouse to put the clipboard back in its place with a sense of accomplishment, like I knew what I was doing, like I was a proper crew member, a proper sailor. Back downstairs, I'm just in time to change into PJs, grab my pillow and blanket, make a cup of tea with a side of toast or a little plastic green cup full of popcorn and find a spot on the floor to make myself comfortable (the big bowl of popcorn within easy reach).

The lights dim, we push play, and we all enjoy the movie and the pleasure of each other's company at the day's end.

Just another normal day.

Constellations

DATE: October 2013
LOCATION: Bay of Biscay
　　　　　45° 37' 30.2" N
　　　　　3° 39' 33.4" W

We were in the beginnings of an ambitious sailing schedule, interrupted by a hurricane farther offshore, forcing us to stop in France to batten down the hatches and get out of its path. In that process, I experienced something I didn't know was a thing – land-sickness. We had been in some rough seas for a while, so when we finally pulled into a port, things were calm again. I had gotten off the ship to go borrow some big ropes from another boat, but by the time I wheeled it back to us, I started to feel queasy. I actually had to get back on the boat, which was still slightly rocking, to ease my stomach. That seemed counterintuitive to me but it worked.

　　Ahead of us we still had to cross the Bay of Biscay through the Strait of Gibraltar, then on to the small island of Gozo. If you've never heard of Gozo, that is absolutely OK. I had never heard of it either until I was told we were going there. Gozo is part of Malta, another very small island just off the coast of Sicily, south of Italy. Basically, it's in the middle of the Mediterranean Sea.

　　One night while we were sailing through the Bay of Biscay, attempting to steer clear of those gale-force winds, I went up to the wheelhouse for my scheduled four-hour night watch. I stepped out on deck to get some fresh air and was greeted by endless stars in every direction. With no land in sight, the only lights besides our own were the ones shining down on us from above. There was one incredibly bright light just in front of our port bow, and I wanted to know its name.

And no, it wasn't the moon ... though I did actually make that mistake once later on ...

With the movement of the ship beneath my feet, I looked straight at that bright light through the darkness and remembered something I had in my cabin that would change the way I saw the night sky forever: an app on my phone that had remained unused for months, just taking up storage space.

When I was home the previous summer, I managed to get a free download of a star app called Sky Guide. You can search for specific stars, planets, constellations, comets even or move it around to discover the names of the stars right above you. The first time I used it, I didn't think much of it, mainly because you can't often see many stars with all the streetlights around. I never used it after that first time, but for some reason, I couldn't find it in me to delete it.

For that, I'm grateful.

I took the trek down to my cabin to grab my phone and opened up the app. I set my location based on our most recent plotted position on the navigational chart. Then, I pointed it directly at the bright light off our port bow.

It was Jupiter.

I began looking at all the other lights just to learn their names. There were the twins, Castor and Pollux, and just next to Jupiter, there was the ever-twinkling Sirius below Regal, Betelgeuse and Bellatrix – the three of them making up the constellation Orion with his belt of three other stars in the middle – and there was the cluster making up the Pleiades. It was all right in front of us. I had never been able to really recognise these shapes in the night sky before. But when you can see it so clearly, it definitely gets a lot easier.

There's nothing quite like sailing through the darkness of night with Jupiter on your port bow and Orion chilling on starboard.

After the discovery of how fantastic this app was, I would get so excited for my night watches just so I could learn more about the stars. Every night as we would start our watch, we'd pray, discuss what to do with the sails, figure out our course, divvy out responsibilities, then out came the star app.

Someone would see a bright light in the distance and ask, 'What's that star?'

I'd walk over to the window, point my phone towards it, and we'd learn about its name, where that name came from, how bright the star was and its distance from us. Each had its own unique story to tell. I loved this newfound ability to see a star in the sky and learn more about it all while just sitting in the wheelhouse among great people, sailing across the sea.

Looking back now, these were the kind of moments that were so sweet. Moments I'll never get again but that are etched into my memories in the most vivid way.

This changed the way I saw the world forever. I could go outside, look up and see more than just white dots scattered randomly across the sky. They were placed there by a really cool God. They had names, faces, facts and figures. They had stories. I could recognise them. They became known to me, like seeing the familiar face of a friend.

I know those stars. I know those constellations. I have confidence that I can look up and immediately see those familiar shapes. I love that I know them.

I had said I wanted to see and know God in everything.

So, I saw God in seeing and knowing the stars.

The Life Jacket

DATE: October 2013
LOCATION: Sail – Brest, France to Viveiro, Spain
44° 24' 9.9" N
6° 31' 21.7" W

Deciding to raise or lower a sail is dependent on a lot of things, some being the force and direction of the wind and what course we wanted to be on. It took a lot of playing around and seeing how the ship reacted to any movement of the sail, whether bringing in the sheets or letting them out.

One particularly beautiful day, the captain gave the order to take the jib down. Even after my not so enjoyable experience with Ben on the sail prior, lowering sails and tying them up was still one of my favourite things to do, apart from helming.

I immediately jumped up, volunteering myself for the task, grabbed a harness and life jacket, and suited up. So did Tamara. With equal enthusiasm. We both went out to the bowsprit as others lowered the halyard and pulled on the down-hauler[18] to get the sail down. I was sitting behind the rigging to help flake it as it came down, and Tamara helped on the other end. With the sail all the way down and in somewhat of a decent flaked position, it was time to tie it up.

As we began the process, I bent over to reach for the line Tamara was handing up to me and when I sat back up, I suddenly heard this extremely loud rush of air surround me. I sat stunned and confused for a moment, having no idea what the heck was going on. It then became very difficult to breathe as my lungs were suddenly and inexplicably constricted, and

---
18 A rope used for hauling down a sail

there was nothing I could do about it. After the initial shock wore off, I figured out what was happened: my life jacket had inflated. Those life jackets were designed to automatically inflate when they hit water. But there was also a pull string at the bottom should it be needed. Well, that string had gotten caught somewhere as I bent down, so sitting back up, it got stuck and the string was pulled.

I just looked at Tamara in utter shock with my hands out to the side, wondering how in the world this just happened. Her reply to my shocked and slightly concerned face was simply laughter. You know you found a good friend when they just laugh when things like this happen to you[19]. I then realised the ridiculousness of the situation, imagining what it must look like to everyone else, and had to laugh myself. There I was, sitting in the middle of the bowsprit over the sea with a big, yellow inflated life jacket suddenly surrounding me. And I could hardly move.

After some of the laughter subsided, I realised that I couldn't do a thing with this life jacket on me. I could hardly breathe, and my movement was incredibly limited. I had tied it around me so tight to begin with that when it inflated, it made it even tighter. But I couldn't figure out how to get even a little air out of it so I could have at least a little mobility, nor how to just get the dang thing off while on the bowsprit which was going up and down.

I needed to get back on deck for some help. I left Tamara to continue packing the sail, hearing her laughter behind me as I hobbled my way off the bowsprit.

We eventually got it off, and it was replaced by another life jacket which I really hoped to not accidentally inflate as I went back out to help Tamara finish the task. I was extra careful in my movements that time.

---

[19] ...the kinds of things like when your lips turn blue after you run a half marathon and your friends are slightly concerned but mostly laughing...

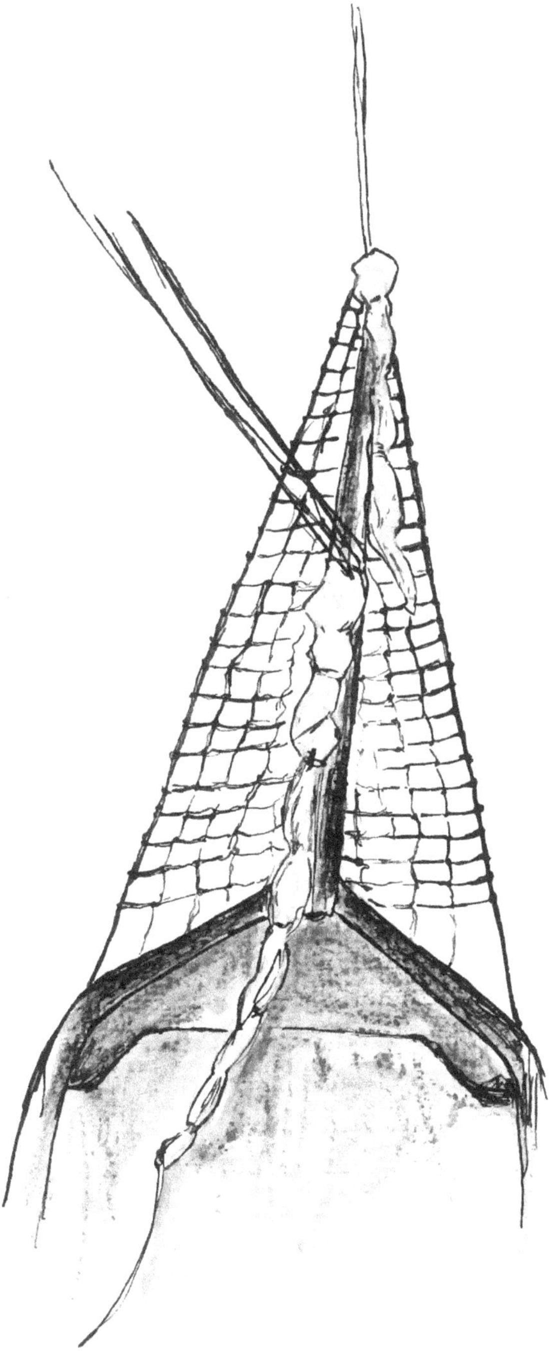

Melodies

You know those songs that when you hear it, it evokes a certain emotion from the very first moment you hear it? The songs that instantly remind you of something? It reminds you of a special time in your life, certain people, places, experiences, memories, emotions, struggles, victories? And you can't help but be taken back to that time in your life?

I have a lot of those songs. One in particular is 'Take Heart' by Hillsong. From the very first second of the introductory melody, I am completely overwhelmed in an instant by such love, calm, peace and goodness. It's not just because of the words of the songs. Yes, they are fantastic lyrics, but there are also mountains of memories tied to this song that I can't ever forget. And I never want to. They are memories of a time living in Room 108 in building number nine on Highfield Oval at YWAM Harpenden with my roommate Sidney. It was a room full of peanut butter and jelly rice cakes, endless YouTube videos (especially that one about a big bunny eating a banana), late night talks and laughs and prayers, a stack of encyclopaedias used as a shelf for our mirror, the big green bean bag, the wood floors, the bird clock, the photos of architectural designs for Westminster Abbey and, my favourite, a picture of a farmer saying 'Dig on for Victory' in addition to a really great friend and roommate. Room 108 was home and will always have such a special place in my heart, no matter how much time passes. When I hear the melody of 'Take Heart' start, I'm instantly taken back to the immense goodness of that time in my life. Just from a few notes on a keyboard.

So, these songs, these melodies, they mean something to us and make us feel something special.

What if it were the same with God?

What if *our* song evoked that same emotion, that same

feeling, that same reminder of immense goodness, in God?

What if our song gave God that same experience?

The song, the melody we bring to God in the way we laugh, the way we run, the way we enjoy life, the way we play, the way we sing, even the way we struggle and cry; each has a special place in God's heart and reminds him of something in us that he created. Something he knows and loves. Something meaningful.

I can live my life knowing that I am loved. Every day I can say that, even on my darkest, ugliest days, I am loved and have done nothing to earn or deserve it. When Jesus was baptised, God said, 'This is my son, whom I love; with him I am well pleased' (Matthew 3:17). God said this before Jesus even began any of his ministry, before he did anything. He just was.

> *The Lord your God is with you,*
> *He is mighty to save.*
> *He will take great delight in you,*
> *He will quiet you with His love,*
> *He will rejoice over you with singing.*
> *Zephaniah 3:17*

He delights in me through all his knowing of me.

Jonathan David Helser once said, 'Worship is giving back to God what He first gave to us.'

God gave you life, he gave you a voice, he gave you movement, he gave you a song to sing and he delights in you when you give that back to him. He delights when you sing him your song with your life. Our living, our worship, can come from a place of wanting to bring delight to the Father. It starts with knowing – I can know that my song delights the Lord. I have done nothing to earn or deserve it, and I don't need to strive to make God happy.

I just need to be, and he delights in that.

Don't Give Up on the First Watch

DATE: *November 2013*
LOCATION: *Bay of Biscay*
45° 37' 30.1" N
3° 39' 33.4" W

The alarm goes off at 07:40.

I hit snooze a couple times then slowly use all my core muscles to hoist myself out of bed on a rocking ship.

I put on my neon green waterproof trousers and step into my wellies.

I grab my coat and head out.

Next, I fill a little green plastic cup with corn flakes and mix in some delicious homemade apple sauce (with my secret ingredient – a touch of bourbon cooked in for added flavour ...).

Then it's up the stairs to the wheelhouse.

The watch passes on to me: I check the sails, confirm the course, we pray, and it begins.

Then comes the feeling that no one enjoys – seasickness. A feeling that I was becoming far too familiar with.

I race to the rail outside on deck and hang out over the side with some not-so-nice things coming back up through my system. There goes my cornflakes and bourbon-infused apple sauce.

I come back in, quite a bit more refreshed (who knew you could feel that much better after throwing up ...), then I grab a piece of toast to restock my stomach.

But then the thought that's always circulating through the depths of my self-critical, self-doubting mind surfaces yet again:

I. CAN'T. DO. THIS.

I don't know what I'm doing.
Or why I'm doing it.
Or how to do it.
I just don't want to do this.
It's hard.
Really hard.
Every moment is a challenge. And kind of sucks sometimes. But this is just the first watch.

There will be the next watch in eight hours' time. Then the next watch. And then the next. And when you're on a four-, five-, or seven-day sail, there's many more next watches to come.

So, what do you do in the midst of that?

In the midst of a storm you have no control over?

In the midst of a squall coming and blowing the sail so hard it snaps a line?

In the midst of not being able to walk in a straight line for a week?

In the midst of constantly yelling at your stomach to just feel better already?

In the midst of the not knowing?

What do you do?

You don't give up.

You keep pushing through because there's another watch to come. There are sails to raise and lower and adjust. There is a course to keep to. There's a watch to finish.

If you give up on the first watch, you miss the dolphins jumping outside, you miss the sunrises and sunsets, you miss watching the stars and knowing their names, you miss the friendship that comes from hanging over the side of a ship with someone who feels just as awful as you do, you miss the laughs and conversations, you miss the adventure, you miss working hard and accomplishing something, you miss the beauty of the moon and its light reflecting on the water.

You miss the right now.

You miss life.

You miss the story.

You miss seeing God in the journey.

I don't want to miss that.

This is just the first watch, and I can't give up.

A Week at Sea

DATE: November 2013
LOCATION: Mediterranean Sea
  37° 10' 40.7" N
  0° 44' 55.2" E

After we had to batten down the hatches in France and Spain to get away from hurricanes in the Bay of Biscay, we found ourselves finally going through the Strait of Gibraltar. It was a gorgeous day so the majority of us were filling every corner of the deck and bowsprit enjoying it. We were looking back and forth from starboard to port because something crazy was happening. On starboard, was Morocco. On port, Spain. Two continents, Africa and Europe, in full view, so close to either side of us as the Rock of Gibraltar came closer into view. We only spent a few days in Gibraltar but I got to hold hands with a monkey (whose initial intent was to steal my water bottle) so it was time well spent.

Most of the sails I had been on up to this point were somewhere between two and four days long. This next one was going to be seven. Seven days. Seven days of just water, no land. Seven days of being on watch for four hours then off for eight hours, then back on for four, off for eight.

One week at sea.

We had a lot of ground to cover and not as much time as we would have liked due to all the delays we had prior. We were pushing hard to travel 1,036 nautical miles from Gibraltar to Gozo in just seven days. Our speed usually averaged between five and seven knots (nautical miles per hour). It all was dependent on the weather and swell. If we managed to keep to those averages, we'd be able to make it in time.

We would also be crossing the prime meridian during this sail, which was more exciting than it might sound. I remember the moment as we closely watched our GPS coordinates change from degrees west to degrees east. It was kind of a big deal.

When you have a watch schedule to keep to, you have to adjust your sleeping and eating patterns in order to accommodate that and be able to be at your best while on watch. While a lazy helmsman made for a good helmsman, a sleepy helmsman was just useless.

On this particular seven-day sail, I had the great fortune of being on the 08:00 – 12:00 / 20:00 – 00:00 watch. This was fortunate because it was the watch that least affected one's normal sleeping patterns. I still felt like a human being on that watch schedule.

As watch leader, I was in charge of not only the practical outworking of actual sailing (which was still crazy to me to have that be part of my job description ...) but also the flow of responsibilities throughout the watch. I wanted everyone on my watch to enjoy it as much as possible. So, my organised self figured out a routine we all could get behind and could stick to for the entire week.

07:30 – Work towards being awake, alert, and clothed appropriately. (OK, so 07:30 might be a stretch ... it more often than not started at 07:45 ...)

08:00 – Our watch gathers up in the wheelhouse, crowded in with the previous watch. I get the rundown on what had been happening, where we're going, and what to prepare for. We pray, and with the previous information in mind, we get to work playing with the sails for a bit as needed.

08:30 – Work duties. Every watch was assigned some kind of work duty, whether cooking a meal or cleaning different areas. Our watch work duties were to clean the toilets and floors. A couple people were assigned to clean those areas while the rest of us stayed up on watch in the wheelhouse, and we would take turns each day.

09:00 – Assign someone to take our current GPS coordinates and plot them on the navigational chart in the navigation office (or just Nav Office for short). Then, it was time for breakfast. Depending on how the ship was rocking, it would either be a very simple breakfast or, if we were lucky and feeling up to the task, Egg in a Poke, which was always a favourite.

10:00 – 12:00 – Assign someone new to plot the position every hour, take turns helming, raising, lowering and setting sails accordingly and spending time in the wheelhouse watching the horizon for other boats and buoys. We always wanted everyone to have the chance of learning all aspects of watchkeeping.

12:00 – 14:00 – We pass the watch off to the next crew, go down to do some stretches in the saloon, then hang out for a bit as more people were awake and moving about. Sometimes this involved me grabbing my guitar and singing some worship songs on deck. Sometimes reading a good book. And sometimes, perfectly rationing and getting the perfect carrot to hummus ratio as my afternoon snack.

14:00 – 17:00 – Nap. This is important. Very important.

17:00 – Start watching a movie while the current watch preps dinner.

18:00 – 20:00 – Eat dinner. Then spend time hanging out either in the saloon or out on deck to watch the sunset. Or nap some more.

20:00 – 00:00 – Back on watch for the night. Weather dependent, stargaze and learn all about them thanks to Sky Guide. Have some of the best conversations in the calm of night on the sea.

00:00 – Pass off the watch, head down to our cabins and get a good night's sleep.

Then, it starts all over.

During one of those evenings just after dinner, we were all sitting outside on deck watching the sunset. I sat next to Tamara near the bow next to the halyard lines coiled up and had an excellent view of the sun falling below the horizon near the starboard quarter[20]. Nearly everyone else had their cameras out trying to capture it. But Tamara and I enjoyed it using the only way to fully take it in – with our eyes.

Suddenly, the sun started to move. Sean had been on the helm and begged the captain if he could have permission to steer in a circle. He wanted to do a full 360-degree rotation then carry on. Permission was more than likely reluctantly granted, but we began to change course. We didn't have any sails up or else this would have been a much more complicated process. As we turned, there was a moment when were quite literally sailing into the sunset. We paused there for a minute to take it all in and then kept turning in the circle until we were back on our intended course and the sun was back where we needed it to be. We were nearing our journey's end.

---

20 The starboard quarter was the back corner of the ship on the starboard side. Port quarter should be self-explanatory...

Thanksgiving

DATE: November 2013
LOCATION: Gozo
   35° 59' 57.4" N
   14° 16' 21.8" E

The ship was always filled with people from all different countries, cultures and holiday traditions. And people who were far from home. We always tried to make holidays on board special. We wanted to make sure everyone had little tastes of home every now and then.

We decided to make a big deal of Thanksgiving. (Let me clarify - American Thanksgiving.) But we were crunched for time. We had to be in Gozo by a certain day because a big group of people would be joining us the following day to stay on board for a week. We wanted to celebrate Thanksgiving with just our community before that happened.

More often than not, Next Wave's weekends never fell on what is usually considered to be a weekend. Holidays often followed suit. I'm not sure exactly what day it was when we celebrated our Thanksgiving, but I'm pretty sure it wasn't the real day that year. The day we chose happened to be a sail day. Challenge accepted.

Tamara and I started the morning in the galley. We had finally made berth in Malta for the night so this was the last stretch of our sail. Neither of us was needed for our mooring operations to get us going, so we took advantage of the time we had to get our supplies out and ready for a day filled with making homemade pie, mashed potatoes and turkey, among other delicious dishes.

A previous endeavour of cooking in the galley while sailing hadn't gone very well. Keeping your balance while trying not to get burnt by a hot stove is really hard and not recommended. But we didn't have a choice. Thankfully, the weather cooperated with us far better than before, so it was much more managcable. And actually, an enjoyable cooking in the galley experience.

About halfway through the day, someone upstairs proposed the idea that we should take a break and have a swim before we arrived in Gozo. During all of our sails, the opportunity had never presented itself for that to happen which was a bummer. Nearly everyone wanted to have that experience before their last sail ended, despite how chilly it was.

The weather wasn't great, but the engines stopped, and we floated around for a bit in between the islands of Malta and Gozo. In the galley, we were thankfully at a good point to pause in our preparations, so I went to get my swimsuit on and ran upstairs to join the fun. When I got out there, they had just finished attaching a thick mooring line to the end of the boom of the mainsail and were in process of rigging it to be out over the water. This was and probably will always be the most epic rope swing I've ever seen.

I grabbed the end of the rope, climbed up on top of the railing and gathered up the courage to jump. I'll be honest, it took me a minute. I've jumped off of high places before, but it always took a little bit of pumping myself up to actually do it. Plus, I knew it was going to be freaking cold. The Mediterranean is always known for its warm, beautiful waters, but in the middle of winter, it does, indeed, get cold.

After several minutes of standing there with everyone yelling at me to stop thinking and just go, I grabbed the rope tight and jumped. Swinging out into the sea, I let go and plummeted into the water.

Coming up for air, Sean yelled down to me, 'How was it?'

All I could manage to say in a shocked, breath-taken-away, high-pitched voice was 'Cold!'

People were swinging on the rope and jumping off the bowsprit until they couldn't handle the cold anymore and we carried on to Gozo. I dried off, changed back into some warm clothes and took my place back in the galley. We had a feast to finish.

Safely docked in Gozo, the ship went quiet with the engines and generators turned off as we connected to shore power. (I had gotten so used to the noise of the generator lulling me to sleep that it took me a while to get used to the quiet.) With the bulk of the cooking nearly completed, the next task was cleaning the saloon and turning it into a beautiful dining area. This was a task because it can get pretty messy during a sail. With everyone dressing up fancy in their cabins, we put the final touches on the presentation of our Thanksgiving feast.

Tables set, mood lighting activated and good food on the table, we enjoyed the beautiful feast after a liturgy written by Daniel:

We have had a safe journey.
Thanks be to God.
We have sailed 2,700 nautical miles.
O God, we give you thanks.
We have finally arrived in Gozo!
We recognise your favour and thank you, Lord
We have had very few injuries
Thank you for your mercy and grace, O Lord
We missed incredibly strong storms all along the way.
We give glory and honour to you, O Lord,
Who watched over us in our journey.
We have grown closer as a community.
Father, we love because you loved first.
We have laughed, thrown up and at times cried out to God together.
You never left us nor forsook us.
We have seen the power and beauty in your creation.
All creation reflects you, our King.

[Pause for reflection, thanking God in our hearts]

We have travelled far, and now our journey is done.
We can join in with the psalmist who says,
'My soul waits for you, as the watchman waits for the dawn.'
We know the yearning for that moment to come.
We earnestly seek you, Lord, and desire your company.
In this night of thanksgiving,
Be welcome at our table.
In this night of reflection,
Be among us.
In this night of community and family,
Share in our fellowship and food.
We welcome you, Lord, into our midst.
We are hungry for more than just food.
May you bless this night as we celebrate.
May you stay in the forefront of our conscious hearts.
May you be blessed by what happens here tonight.
May you smile as we smile.
May you enjoy as we enjoy.

We love you, Lord.

In the name of the Father and the Son and the Holy Spirit.
Amen.

Orion

DATE: December 2013
LOCATION: Gozo
            36° 1' 38.5" N
            14° 18' 16.4" E

I love exploring and finding beautiful places to walk and sit and enjoy the surroundings. I found a great path in Gozo just a quick walk from where the ship was berthed in the middle of Mgarr Marina at the base of a village called Ghajnsielem (say it with me...Ine-see-lem ... roughly ...). It's a path that went along the water's edge of this gorgeous little island. It's a place I visited often.

One night, my emotions were high, so I ran off the ship and headed for this path in the night. I didn't want to go too far so I stopped at a rock looking back at the marina with the moon shining above me. After I got most of my emotions out, I looked up to the left of the moon and saw Orion in the clear night sky.

Once you learn to recognise Orion, you can't not see it when you look up.

I turned to face away from the moon and gazed at the stars surrounding me. That's the thing about being in places with little to no lights at night, the stars get to show off a whole lot more. I spotted Jupiter and the Pleiades and out came the star app again. I learned about seven new constellations that night. They were all right in front of me.

But Orion. I had come to recognise and know Orion better than all the rest. I guess keeping Orion on the starboard bow through the night really solidified that.

With a more level (and star savvy) headspace, I walked back along the water to the ship. On this walk, God said something to me that I would not soon forget.

He said, 'You are going to know so much more of my goodness.'

I held on to that as a promise. I wasn't loving who I had become in the circumstances I was living. I felt angry and upset more often than not coming out of the stress that my first months back on board had brought when we were stuck. Plus, living on a boat was just hard to do in general. Really hard. It's easy to talk about all the good things, the fun things, the outrageous and adventurous things. But it's harder to talk about the hard things. I felt like I wasn't allowed to be having a hard time living on a boat. I kept thinking, Look at the amazing places you're going, the incredible experiences you're having, the great people around you. Just be happier. Just do better. Just be better. I often felt that I was doing everything wrong.

But I've found that we can't force ourselves to be happier in life's circumstances. We can't will ourselves to love every bit of where we're at and what we're doing and who we're doing it with all the time. It takes work. For me, it took many, many, many walks along the water to start seeing that there might possibly be a point to all of it. But I also knew it would take a while for me to see and know that point, to see and know that purpose. It might even take years.

So, when God told me I was going to know so much more of his goodness that night, I held on tight to it. I beat that into my chest. I reminded myself of it every single day. And on the days I couldn't see it, on the days I couldn't believe it, God would remind me.

Another night, about a week later, I headed in the opposite direction of my usual path. I walked through the marina, passed the colourful boats that are so iconically Gozo tied together in the water, passed Horatio's pub, by the ferry terminal and to the edge of the parking lot. There wasn't much of a path that I could see though. (I tended to go on these walks at night so light was limited, especially since I hardly brought my phone to be able to use as a flashlight on these walks.) I climbed down along the rocks to find a good sitting place closer to the water. The sound of water crashing up on the rocks was always a soothing sound I could listen to for hours, kind of like staring at a fire.

It was a cloudy night. The grey clouds covered the entire sky, so it was impossible to see the stars at all. I could hardly make out where the moon was, though I knew it was up there somewhere. A little disappointed with that, I started talking to God about my frustrations. He had said I was going to know more of his goodness, but that day I just couldn't believe it. He had said he would be with me, but that day I couldn't feel it.

With what appeared to be the silent treatment, I gave up talking. I gave up hoping for an answer. But then I looked up again. I had no reason to look up because I knew all there was to see was the grey covering of the clouds across the sky.

But I looked up anyways and saw a small, clear break in the clouds right in front of me in the exact place I looked up to. When I saw what was in that clearing, I burst into tears.

It was Orion.

But not just part of him. All of him. And it was perfectly centred right in the middle of that small break in the clouds. It only lasted a moment until the clouds took over the clearing again.

It was another moment of knowing that it could only have been God that made that moment happen.

I'm not saying that everything was all better after this moment. That all of a sudden, all was right within me. If only it were ever that easy. But it was the reminder I needed to keep looking up, to keep hoping and trusting in the promises God had made. A glimpse of his goodness in my life. A reminder that he was always with me even if I didn't believe it or feel it. A reminder that told me that God wanted me to see more than just part of his goodness, more than just part of who is.

He saw me that night, sitting on those rocks, upset, angry, hurting. He opened up the clouds so I could see something familiar, something that brought comfort because I knew it. I knew the shape of Orion. I could recognise it beyond a shadow of a doubt.

God wants us, when we look up, to see something familiar. He wants us to see him and know him. To recognise him in and through our lives beyond a shadow of a doubt. And he is so persistent in our imperfect, annoyingly inconsistent ways. He is persistent in showing that he loves us and that his goodness surrounds us.

Once you recognise God in your life, you can't not see him when you look up.

Surely goodness and love will follow me
all the days of my life,
and I will dwell in the house of the Lord forever.
Psalm 23:6

The constellations are always there. They always have been and always will be. But a lot of times, they're not easily seen or recognised. Sometimes because you literally can't see them, though more often because it takes time to make out the shapes.

But once you start to see those shapes, it all comes together and they're easy to see.

But you have to look. You have to seek it out again and again to come to a point of recognising those shapes all around.

God is always good. He always has been and always will be. His goodness is all around, but it sometimes takes a while to really see it, to really know it. We need a lot of reminders about it. But through it all, you get to see and know that he's good.

You have to say yes to the invitation to see and know. And trust that he'll show you.

How can one tell of the beauty that's before me?
How vast the expanse across the skies,
My eyes can't take it all in at once.
How can one tell of the beauty that's before me?
The lights by which men of old have travelled.
My mind can't comprehend the splendour.

In all of this
I see
The One looking back at me.
In all of this
I know
The goodness of One who created me.

How can one tell of the beauty that's before me?
Through the roughest seas and the darkest storms
It forever surrounds me.
How can one tell of the beauty that's before me?
The shapes once unable to distinguish
Now the shapes so familiar.

In all of this
I see
The One looking back at me
In all of this
I know
The goodness of One who created me.

Thank You
Thank you for your goodness unable to tell.

Part 3
TO FEEL HIS ABSENCE

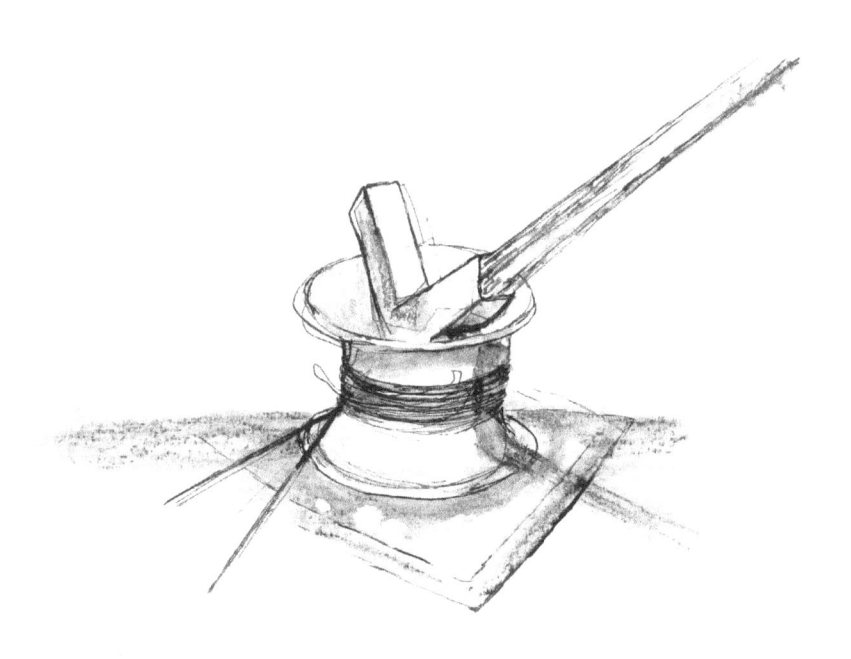

January 2014 – April 2014

Gozo, Malta – Piraeus, Greece: 9 days, 621 nm
Piraeus, Greece – Mykonos – Patmos – Kos – Rhodes, Greece: 7 days, 305 nm
Rhodes, Greece – Larnaca, Cyprus: 4 days, 328 nm
Larnaca, Cyprus – Paphos, Cyprus: 3 days, 146 nm
Paphos, Cyprus – Herzliya, Israel: 3 days, 215 nm
Herzliya, Israel – Mersin, Turkey: 4 days, 305 nm

Surviving the Squall

DATE: January 2014
LOCATION: Ionian Sea
        38° 5' 55.5" N
        18° 32' 57.9" E

We set out from Gozo on a beautiful Mediterranean afternoon. We hoisted all five sails then cut the engine. We were properly sailing. We were heeled over on a starboard tack. So much so at times that we were almost walking on the walls down in the saloon. It was a challenge to get out of bed (or stay in bed depending on what side of the boat your bed was on and the direction it faced ...). One's centre of gravity tends to change quite a bit when one is perpetually leaning for a long period of time.

Then, things began to change.

The wind started to pick up and so did the swell. The boat was moving like I'd never felt before. Due to our rapid ascending and descending each wave, I started to feel the beginning stages of seasickness. Despite the disciplined regimen I had created to combat that seasickness, my spaghetti from the night before wasn't sitting too well. (You'd think I would have learned by then to not eat anything tomato-related before or during a sail ...) So, I went outside to sit and get some fresh air to calm my stomach. I sat out on the port side of the wheelhouse so I could have something to lean back against. I was tired of using every ab muscle I possessed to stay upright. Jasmine and Zhenya joined me. It's always better to struggle through feeling like crap with others by your side, right? The rocking continued and then it started to drizzle a bit. Then, it started to rain harder.

And harder.

And harder.

The winds picked up strong with that heavy rainfall. The sky turned dark with thick grey clouds.

Hello, squall.

A squall can be defined as such: a sudden violent gust of wind of brief duration, a short-lived commotion, a sudden disturbance.

That definition honestly sounds less intense than it actually is when you're in the middle of it.

Jasmine, who shared a cabin with me on the deck just below where we were sitting, suddenly yelled out, 'The porthole!'

She shot up to her feet and raced down the steep steps from the wheelhouse, passed the galley, down the crew hallway, and into the first door on the right to our cabin before I could register what could possibly be happening.

Before every sail, we had an extensive time of securing the ship for sail. This meant tying things together, latching all doors, and putting everything away. Living on a ship, you had to think and assume that any and everything could and would fall at any given time, so you always needed to secure it to avoid breakage. One aspect of securing the ship was always closing the portholes. Seawater splashing in through a porthole is not an ideal situation. I know because it happened to me in the galley that one time. So, before we set sail, I made sure our cabin porthole was closed and secure.

When Jasmine ran away exclaiming about the porthole with the ship heeling over farther and farther, I couldn't imagine why she would be freaking out about it. I had secured the porthole myself before we began our journey. But apparently, she had opened it earlier in the day without my knowledge when the weather was nice to air out our cabin and had just forgotten to close it.

As she reached our cabin door, our porthole was completely submerged below the water line and a wave of seawater was pouring in, soaking our beds and shelves, sloshing on the floor. Outside, the winds were gusting against the sails, the ship heeled over so far that the water line was suddenly above the windows of the deck below (hence the wave of water in our cabin). We were pushed over even more to the point of the main deck reaching the surface of the water on the port side. By this time, I was standing nearly straight up on the railings of the deck, pushing hard against the wall of the wheelhouse to hold me up and back from the approaching waters. The sea began to creep up on deck, surrounding my feet almost up to my shins. I decided it was time to go back inside. I suddenly was over my seasickness and knew it was time to get to work as we bounced back upright. The ship was designed to always bounce back and for that I was grateful.

I quickly put on my wet weather gear, after seeing the aftermath of the wave of water in our cabin, and went on deck to see where I could help. We had to get the sails down and fast. The squall was still with us (so much for 'brief duration' ...), and things were more dangerous with canvas up. I somehow kept my calm as we went from one sail to the other to lower them and coil the ropes, making sure the other passengers were doing alright (whom this was their first (and possibly only) sail ever, unfortunately) and everything could be secured. After half an hour of this crazy squall, it finally died down and the sun returned along with blue skies. It was gone like it was trying to trick us into thinking it had never even happened.

We were tired. So, we had lunch.

My next watch began at 16:00, and things were looking better. We called ourselves 'The Ladies of the Bridge'. I hand-picked my watch team of five because I just thought they were all really cool ladies, and I wanted to spend time with them. And we were an excellent watch team if I do say so myself. We were doing all our watch duties and enjoying who were doing it with. Our watch passed without issue.

01:00 hit, and we were suddenly immersed in a full-on gale – somewhere between a Force 7 and Force 10 on the Beaufort Scale[21]. This meant wind gusts between thirty and fifty miles per hour with high waves cresting on either side of us, the sea spray soaking every bit of our deck and sails and selves. Quite a bit more intense than the squall before. And worse because it was in the middle of the night. I had been sleeping and was woken up by all the intense noise above me. Right when I got up to the wheelhouse to see what was going on, I bolted outside to throw up what was left of my dinner. I felt awful and was not up for helping. I knew that if I stepped foot on deck in my tired, seasick state, I would be more risk than help.

So, I watched. Helpless. Anxious. Worried. Afraid.

Deep darkness engulfed us as the deck lights revealed only a portion of what was going on around us. Not even the moon was out to aid our light. I watched as they lowered all the sails in a hurry, everyone in life jackets and harnesses strapped to the safety lines roped across the deck. I watched as ropes flailed in the wind, as sails flapped heavily on their way down, the boat rocking side to side, rains pounding on everyone and wind rushing through. I watched as people crawled across the deck, struggling to tie down and secure the sails. I watched as Thomas

---

21 The Beaufort scale is a scale of wind speed that can be based on the visual effects of the wind on the water

came back inside, sitting down on the floor in utter exhaustion after having held fast the sails out on the bow.

With all the sails down and secure enough, we motored on through the rest of the night. Surprisingly, through all this, the engine had no problems, so we could keep moving. And praise God no one was hurt throughout the ordeal. I went back to my cabin to try to get a couple hours' sleep before my next watch was to begin at 04:00.

Later the next afternoon, we raised the massive flying jib, the foremost sail, and things were going pretty well, our speed getting up to nine knots, the usual average being maybe four or five. The Ladies of the Bridge were pretty proud of ourselves for that. The sun was setting beautifully, and we were all smiles as we finished our dinner, and I was hopeful the worst was behind us.

I was wrong.

That storm had done a lot of damage to us. One thing that I and a couple of my ladies on watch had to take care of that afternoon was detaching the mizzen[22] sail completely off the aft boom. The sail itself, which had just been repaired, tore again from the force of the wind the previous night making it useless and in need of further repair. Can't really catch much wind in a sail with a big hole in the middle. The bigger issue was that the boom had somehow detached itself from the mast. How that happened, I will never know or understand because those are some pretty heavy-duty nuts and bolts to keep the extremely heavy beam of solid wood in place. It somehow had lifted up and out of place which put it at the risk of just sliding right off the back of the boat into the water to be lost forever. We had to detach the sail and secure both the canvas and the boom to the roof of the wheelhouse so we wouldn't lose either, and we planned to repair it later in port when we were settled.

---

22 A sail at the back of the boat.

We had almost finished getting the sail loose from the boom, preparing to tie it down and secure it to the roof, when the winds started to pick up again. The flying jib we were earlier so proud to see fly high started thundering in the wind, which is a sound I had come to dread. Not only was the incredibly loud crack of the sail hard against the wind enough to terrify anyone, it also shook the entire boat with a force that was hard to comprehend.

Another squall. Another sudden disturbance. No rain this time, which I guess was better, right? Well, not quite. We were suddenly surrounded again by black clouds and fierce winds. That jib needed to come down and fast at the risk of doing some serious damage, more than had already been done.

One major problem – four out of the six Ladies of the Bridge were up on the wheelhouse with a loose and unsecured boom and mizzen sail, holding on tight so we wouldn't lose it to the sea, one was doing engine checks down below in the engine room, and the other was on the helm keeping our course. This left no one on deck to take down the sail.

The thunderous sounds and shaking of the entire boat left me frozen on top of the wheelhouse in the middle of it all. I didn't know what to do. I was responsible for the safety of this watch, and I couldn't move. The other ladies went from watching and listening to the sail crack on the lines to looking at me with worried looks on their faces, the wind roaring through our ears. Intense fear overtook me, and all I could do was watch and pray it would stop.

But it didn't. Not soon enough anyways.

I prayed for the winds to cease, I asked God to show up and take care of us. I pleaded with him to calm the storm.

But he didn't. Not soon enough anyways.

My internal cries going seemingly unanswered, I felt utterly alone. Here we were in the middle of this horrible storm, sitting out in the open to the elements, and God was nowhere to be found. I suddenly came to understand why the disciples freaked out so much when they found themselves in a storm and Jesus was sleeping through it (Mark 4:35-41).

I had never felt more abandoned by God. I had never felt his absence as much as in that moment.

Within a couple minutes, which felt like hours to me, others began appearing on deck, responding to the thunderous sounds that could be heard and felt throughout the entire ship. I watched as they raced to start rolling in the flying jib. With crew members on the lines, I awoke out of my frozen state, and we continued our initial task of detaching the mizzen sail and securing the boom so we could get off the roof of the wheelhouse.

We sat in silence inside until 20:00 when our watch had ended. We had been motoring through the choppy seas for the remainder of our watch, trying with all our might to keep upright.

When the next watch was passed on to me the following morning, I told the rest of the Ladies of the Bridge that we were going to try to take things easy for our next few watches until we reached our destination. We'd all do the typical duties of engine checks, watching for other ships or buoys in the distance, and take turns helming and plotting our position on the chart every hour. But I wasn't up for playing with the sails. Everyone agreed to that.

The best thing about the 04:00–08:00 / 16:00–20:00 watch was that you got to see both the sunrise and the sunset. The sun rose to greet us that morning and brought with it a little hope and certainly some much-needed calm. The Ladies enjoyed each other's company through sharing a meal, swapping stories and attempting to loosely translate what we would occasionally hear being spoken between other boats over the radio in very unknown languages. (Though one instance was actually in English and could be fully understood, so the 'translation' was not entirely accurate, or a translation at all. We had a good laugh about that one when I said, 'umm, actually, this is what they just said'...)

After a gloomy week on board through indecisive weather, we finally made it to a safe haven near land where were dropped anchor. We weren't quite to our end destination but we took the chance to just stop and rest.

We just didn't anticipate being stopped for so long.

Stuck at Anchor

DATE: *February 2014*
LOCATION: *Somewhere near the coast of Greece ...*

The next morning, we woke up to attempt fixing whatever the storm had destroyed. We had to raise and re-lower the mainsail as it was a complete mess and was falling out all over the place. This was when we discovered the boom had been bent significantly right in the middle. This was a big hunk of metal that now had a massive kink in it. Those were some fierce winds to have achieved that kind of thing. The mizzen boom also had to be reattached to the mast; lines had to be checked for damage and recoiled. The list was long.

We then came to find out that we were somehow unable to hoist the anchor. Our hydraulics weren't working. Probably another thing to get messed up by this storm. We were quite literally stuck. That's not the best feeling. I'm not a fan of being stuck. I had learned that fact about myself from being stuck in Glasgow *and* Birkenhead, so it was a familiar yet very unwelcome feeling. I'm definitely not at my best when I feel stuck. But we had been in port those other times. This time, we were out at sea with no access to land. Cabin fever is a real thing and I felt it.

To cope that afternoon, I borrowed a hammock, grabbed my iPod and favourite fleece blanket, put on a harness, and made my way to the foredeck. I attached myself to the safety line on the bowsprit and climbed out onto the net. I carefully tied my blanket tight to the net so it wouldn't fly away and be lost to the sea, made sure my pockets were securely zipped so as not to lose my iPod, and attached the hammock underneath the net as far out to the tip as I could go.

Then came the conundrum of figuring out how to actually climb down into the hammock without falling to the sea below. Yes, I was attached to the net with my harness on, but it was still a risky manoeuvre. Similar to getting down off the crow's nest, I just had to go for it and hope for the best, trusting my arm strength and manoeuvrability. It all proved trustworthy, and I made it in the hammock and bundled up in my blanket. In went the earphones, and I finally had a moment to actually rest and relax. It was a bit chilly and windy but, in that moment, I didn't care. I was away from everyone, as far as I could physically get, and I could breathe for just a second. My introverted self was getting a small portion of the recharge it needed.

As I was relaxing out there under the net of the bowsprit (which is quite high off the water level), I saw Thomas coming with a harness and the bosun's chair. I just watched from below as he rigged himself to be hoisted up towards the sheets of the flying jib to untangle them as they had been incredibly knotted around each other during the storm, making them unusable. Thomas was quite the monkey when it came to the ship's rigging. It was fun to watch from the comfort of my hammock. I stayed out there until it was too cold and windy for my liking.

During this time that we were stuck, we ran out of salt. Because we couldn't just have one thing go wrong at a time. That's not a good thing when you are cooking for a lot of people. We went through a lot of salt. Salt added necessary flavour to all our meals, so without it, things would have been rather tasteless. When people eat good food, they are generally happier people. So, to be out of salt could have resulted in less happy people than we already had, considering our present circumstances. The only way to remedy this situation was to make our own.

Zhenya took on this task. She attached a bucket to a line and threw it into the sea to scoop up some seawater. She then spent hours and hours boiling it over the stove until the water completely evaporated and all that was left was sea salt. There might have been more involved in the process, but this is what I gathered happened. All I knew was that for dinner that night, there was salt. The freshest Mediterranean Sea salt I had ever had and probably will ever have.

We were stuck in a small bay right off the coast of Greece. So, what does one do in that situation when there is a break in the day?

Jump ship.

I had only jumped off of the ship once or twice before, and I had talked about it a lot with the new team we had with us, this being their first time on a boat (what an introduction ...). We discussed it and agreed we would do it after lunch. But it was during our morning tea break when this was discussed, and we were already all on deck enjoying our tea and biscuits and it was sunny. I had recognised a trend with the weather over the previous couple of days that it was nice in the morning and then it got cold, cloudy, and windy by the afternoon. I knew that come lunchtime, I probably wouldn't want to go swimming. I made the executive decision to go downstairs, put my swimming gear on, and jump off the bowsprit at tea break instead.

Others followed suit at my invitation.

Sometimes impulsive decisions are the best decisions.

We were stuck in a really frustrating situation that nobody expected, anticipated or wanted to be in which lasted much longer than anyone would have preferred. A situation I was getting all too familiar with. I learned the hard way that in situations like that, you *have* to do something to find life. You have to do something that adds joy to the situation and gets people out of their justifiable negativity.

I came up, ready to go, along with a good number of others, and we made a line along the net of the bowsprit to jump into the water.

I was first in line. If I was going to be a leader, these were the kinds of things I wanted to lead people into.

Now, may I remind you that while I was in a country in the middle of the Mediterranean Sea known for its wonderful weather, it was the end of January at the time, which equalled winter. Winter is a chilly season, no matter where in the world you are. That water was the kind of cold that takes your breath away immediately when you are submerged.

We all had our breath taken away in the best of ways that tea break.

It was so much fun to jump from that height and then to see others conquer their fears in doing the same. To see them climb up the ladder back on deck with a huge smile on their face. We were still in a crappy situation, but for that moment, life was good and the joy was contagious.

One of my more memorable morning tea breaks, among many.

———⤎⤎———

After a couple days of being stuck at anchor, working all day on repairs, an idea was hatched to figure out a way to get us moving again. The only other option besides cutting it off and leaving it behind was to lift the heavy anchor by hand.

Which we did. (Well, *they* did.)

For at least six hours.

It was a lot of work that could only be done one little bit at a time.

How this worked was our engineer, along with the help of several others, managed to rig a way of passing a hook down through the hole in the bow along the anchor chain to someone on the water in the dinghy who would attach the hook to the heavy chain. This rope was strung up the mast, through a block (pulley), back down to the main deck, and around a capstan[23]. Four people, using two capstan poles[24], two people on each pole, pushed forward clockwise with all their might around and around, another sitting on the ground helping to pull the line and raise the anchor chain. It could only go a few metres until the rotating would have to stop and the chain locked in place. Then, the hook was lowered back to the waterline and the process began again and would be repeated over and over and over. For six hours.

I somehow got out of the majority of the heavy working on the capstan due to having a somewhat minor injury that I may or may not have exaggerated the pain level of so as to be able to offer my services to the captain during that time instead. (I'll just admit it ... my finger hurt. And I needed a Band-Aid. That was it. I know, pathetic. I was just kind of done with all the things at that point and didn't care.) His job for me was to sit somewhat

---

23 A mechanical rotating device on the deck of a ship to aid in hauling, winding, and holding ropes. See title page for Part 3 for a visual.
24 Poles that are inserted into the capstan to be used to turn it.

comfortably on the bowsprit and tell him the angle of the anchor chain so he could manoeuvre the ship accordingly. Depending on the angle of the chain, it would either be easier or harder for the others to lift due to its tension. We wanted to make it easier on everyone. As they pulled in the chain, we would have to move forward towards where the anchor was resting on the seafloor to loosen its strain.

Well done to those of you who did the actual hard work the majority of the time. My apologies for being a lazy wimp that day. We all have those days though, right?

It was a bit chilly sitting out there on the bowsprit, but that's the price I paid for my laziness. One of my beloved Ladies of the Bridge was a gem and made me a cup of tea while I sat out there in the cold wind with the sun slowly fading from view behind the hills along with its heat. I kept Thomas somewhat entertained while he was in the dinghy in charge of attaching the hook as it came down to him. Someone even decided it would be more comfortable for me out on the bowsprit net to have the bosun's chair to sit on. That was a great idea as for an extended time (or any amount of time, really) that net is not the most comfortable place to sit.

It was a nice enough day though, and we brought out the speakers to put some music on while Jasmine and Zhenya sat on deck with cutting boards, big bowls and potato peelers preparing our well-deserved dinner. Well, *their* well-deserved dinner.

After the anchor was finally off the seafloor, my job was done and I was able to get off the bowsprit and warm up. My only choice to warm up was to finally help on the capstan. I felt I owed it to those who actually did the work. And let me tell you, it wasn't easy.

With everyone working together, they managed to get the anchor up with a great shout of victory, and off we went for another seventeen-hour journey to Piraeus, the port of Athens, which was our original intended destination.

This final push to Piraeus was easy, which everyone was extremely thankful for. No squalls. As we set our course for Piraeus, we watched the sun set beautifully and were welcomed to the city in the morning with a gorgeous sunrise.

Not more than twenty feet walking away from the ship into the marina after we arrived, I looked back and thought, *This is the farthest distance I've walked in nine days.*

I was happy to be on land again.

Eating in Foreign Countries

DATE: February 2014
LOCATION: Piraeus, Greece
37° 55' 52.6" N
23° 38' 51.8" E

One of the biggest challenges with travelling around the world is the ever-present language barrier. And when you continually move from country to country, each with their own native language, some confusion is inevitable.

Greek is an interesting language because not only is it rather difficult to understand upon hearing, but written, it is comprised of incredibly unfamiliar characters. To one having no understanding of the Greek language, absolutely nothing makes sense.

Jasmine was the galley manager at the time and was in charge of not only planning and preparing all of our meals but also shopping for the food. That was quite the task as it required planning meals on a tight budget for an ever-changing number of people, some with a plethora of dietary restrictions (myself included) as well as shopping in foreign countries which meant locating the nearest grocery store with foreign ingredients, language and currency. It's a lot to handle. I say all of this to preface this story in defence of Jasmine for the events that transpired.

Jasmine and Zhenya had gone to Carrefour, the local grocery store, which was a good thirty-minute walk away from where we were berthed (sometimes it takes a while to navigate out of the marina into town) to do the shopping for a group of twenty-some people who had just had quite the epic sailing experience, and we were close to nearly running out of food. We were certainly out of salt. They had their list, shopping bags ready and went to work, perusing through the aisles to get all they needed. Unpacking the carts onto the conveyor belt to check out, Jasmine realised she forgot something of vital importance: meat for that evening's meal. She ran to the meat section, grabbed something quickly off the shelf and raced back to Zhenya in time to finish the transaction. From there, they made the long trek back with heavy packs on their backs and full carrier bags in each hand. Carrying that amount of food for that great distance is no small feat. (Later on, we discovered we could actually take our dinghy all the way to the main entrance of that store and motor it all back which proved to be a much more efficient and less strenuous way of doing it. But that was discovered after this day, unfortunately.)

The cooking commenced in the galley which was often the place many people congregated despite its lack of space. I think a kitchen of any kind tends to have that draw for people. And spending time with friends surrounded by the sounds and smells of something delicious cooking was always enjoyable. I would often walk in the door and sit on the wooden lid of the rubbish bin next to the refrigerator, warming up with the electric towel rack behind me, watching the chefs at work, listening to good music and just chatting about anything and everything. This day, I walked in to take my usual perch to find laughter echoing in the hidden corner of the galley. Curious, I walked in farther to peek my head around.

Jasmine looked at me hesitantly, hiding behind her smile. 'Umm, will you come over here and smell this? It, uhh, doesn't really smell like chicken.'

I reluctantly stepped towards the stove and inhaled a smell that was oddly familiar but couldn't quite put words to. Or rather, I was afraid to put words to it at the risk of my being right.

I eyed her suspiciously without saying a word when she asked again, "What do you think it smells like?'

With concerned confusion on my face, I leaned in again and sure enough, my initial instinct of what I thought it smelled like was seemingly becoming more correct. I honestly thought it smelled a little bit like, dare I say it, urine.

Wide-eyed and in shock, I asked, 'What the heck are you cooking?'

She laughed and reluctantly answered, 'What if I were to tell you that we're cooking a, uhh, naughty part of the pig?'

'Ummm ... what part of the pig??'

'They're... uh ... pig testicles.'

'Are you serious?!'

'Yep.' She quietly replied with her Jasmine smile.

I looked back to Zhenya who was busying herself on the other side of the galley preparing vegetables with a huge smirk on her face, trying to hold in the laughs. I looked back to Jasmine and then the meat and then Jasmine again, still in slight shock and not knowing how to react to that kind of information. Realising the ridiculousness of the situation and its reality setting in, I caught their contagious laughter. Others came in to ask what was so funny, but not another word about it was spoken. I just walked out holding my breath as if nothing was wrong, though it all seemed very wrong.

Sitting down to eat, I kept glancing between Zhenya and Jasmine as everyone dished up their meal family style. I looked at my plate, nearly gagging at the thought of what I was about to consume. I mean, Jasmine knows her spices, so it looked and smelled amazing. But I still knew the truth. I didn't want to make a big deal of it and spill the beans so in it went.

Surprisingly, it wasn't the worst thing I've ever tasted. Initial bites were uncomfortable as I knew exactly what I was chewing, but if I just ignored that vital piece of information, I could get through it. Not something I'd ever willingly eat again though. Funny enough, that particular meal received a surprising number of compliments across the saloon. With every compliment made, a bigger smile appeared on the faces of us who knew exactly what they were complimenting.

About a month later, we were in Cyprus. The DTS had returned from outreach, and we were having a night of testimonies. The DTS were presenting stories of what they had done while on outreach and us crew members presented stories of what we had gotten up to on board, which included beautiful sails and swimming in the sea throughout Greece and, of course, the squall. Another story also came out: the story of eating pig testicles.

Jasmine and Zhenya had prepared a very accurate re-enactment of how the events transpired, and by the end of the sketch, they revealed to the rest of the crew that they had, in fact, all eaten pig testicles while in Greece. Thomas was the most shocked out of everyone. He had thought the re-enactment was just a joke the whole time as they were acting it out, and when it finally hit him that they were serious, he was in disbelief.

We all had a good laugh while also apologising to those crew members that this was how they had to find out.

*I would like to extend a further apology to those of you who may have realised through reading this story that you were on board during this particular dinner in Piraeus (you may also remember the orange biscuits ...) and that you have unfortunately also eaten pig testicles without knowing it due to our very intentional lack of communication.

This Is Where I Have You

DATE: *February 2014*
LOCATION: *Piraeus, Greece*
  $37°\ 55'\ 52.6"\ N$
  $23°\ 38'\ 51.8"\ E$

There are times in life when you just want to give up. There are a lot of those times. When things aren't going like you want them to and it all just seems pretty awful, giving up often sounds like the best option. But sometimes, you can't do anything about it and have to hold fast.

There were countless times during that squall-filled sail and the days stuck at anchor when I was filled with so much fear and frustration and all I wanted to do was be done and give up. But there was literally nowhere I could go – there was no way that I could give up. It just wasn't even an option I could seriously consider. We were all pushed to our breaking points and then some, but we kept going and made it through. Because we had to.

Looking back, I know that experience strengthened me so much more than I realised, but in that moment, I just wanted to be done. I wanted, I needed to get off the boat for a little bit to have a break, to attempt to have space to breathe. If we're not allowed to give up, we're at least allowed a break every once in a while.

A couple days after we arrived in Piraeus, I booked a flight to hop over to another city on the northeast side of Greece called Thessaloniki to visit the DTS team there on outreach. And to give my best friend a hug.

They had no idea I was coming, so I got to give the ultimate surprise when I showed up for dinner that night. To be welcomed with such love was so wonderful. I got to jump in on some of the outreaches they were doing and just catch up with them. It had been almost two months since I'd seen them, so it did my heart good to be among old friends.

On my last night with the DTS in Greece, Tamara and I took the evening to go have dinner. It was long overdue for us to be able to spend quality time together since she'd been away for a while. I had missed our wine dates greatly. We feasted on tabbouleh, falafels, portobello mushrooms and homemade wine in really cool bottles. If I was going to be in Greece, I needed to eat and drink as they did, and it did not disappoint. But I couldn't say the same for our conversation.

The thing about YWAM is that things can change real quick. Nothing could prepare me for the change I was about to be hit with. Daniel and Tamara decided to step down as the directors of Next Wave at the end of the DTS they were leading to pursue a new direction. That meant that in less than two months, my best friend would be leaving.

I was devastated.

It's easy to be incredibly selfish when you're already feeling down, alone and discouraged and then someone close to you decides to move forward with new and good things in their lives. My initial reaction was out of pure selfishness. I was happy for them about where they'd be going but I was also very selfishly bummed. I didn't want my best friend to leave. I cried all the way back to the ship the next day, throughout the whole flight and the long walk back through town.

In my stressed-out state, I reached out to a few very important people in my life for some guidance. I felt I had a big decision to make that I wasn't thrilled about. It was a decision I had been contemplating for a bit, but it came to a head in

Greece. I was deciding between giving up, leaving, going home or finishing out a commitment I had made to the ship and to myself and to God.

One of those important people was Jessica. She always had this way of pointing me back to the Lord no matter what the situation was. She reminded me of that over and over for years. And still does to this day. She encouraged me that I needed a fresh word from the Lord. I was frustrated with that at first because I knew it was true, but I was also mad at him for the whole situation I was in so I didn't want to ask. I felt like we just weren't on the best of terms considering that whole squall thing and feeling like he just kinda left.

I hung up my Skype call with Jessica and, on my walk back to the ship from the café, I got that fresh word. But I didn't like what he had to say.

'This is where I have you.'

I hated that. I was mad at that. I didn't want this to be where God wanted me to be. I was tired of it. It was hard. But that's what it was, without a doubt. I cried some more. I may have had that fresh word from the Lord about where he wanted me to be, but I certainly wasn't thrilled about it.

I was ready to jump ship. Actually, this time. I was ready to just give up and go home. I didn't care that God may have wanted me to be there. I didn't want to be there. I was tired and burnt out and ready to be done.

I needed to take a longer break from the ship than just five short days. I needed to get to England. I needed to go back to my favourite place with its fields and footpaths and tea and crumpets and old friends. I needed space. Actual space. I needed to process what was going on and re-evaluate my decisions and what I was doing with my life.

But I couldn't afford it. I had no money in my bank account. I sat at a café one afternoon looking at flights in tears because there was no way I could pay for a ticket. With compassion, a dear fellow crew member looked at me from across the table and offered to pay for my flight to England. I couldn't believe it. I was so grateful. She bought my ticket, and I felt relief knowing that I would soon get to go back to England. It wouldn't be for another two months, but I knew I could push through until then.

Bean Warriors

DATE: *February 2014*
LOCATION: *Patmos, Greece*
37° 19' 49.6" N
26° 33' 28.2" E

After our few weeks in Piraeus, we began our leisurely journey island hopping the Greek Islands on our way to Cyprus, just us crew. Those were some of the most beautiful sails I went on. The weather was perfect and beautiful. The water, still. We would anchor in a bay just off the coast, allowing for time to explore the island for the day before heading out to the next one. (Don't worry, our hydraulics were back in working order so we could raise and lower the anchor at will again.)

We always had to have at least one person on duty on the ship every day. So, one day, after dropping everyone off on the island, I motored the dinghy back to Next Wave, and was on my own on this big ship in a bay off the coast of Greece. So, I popped a bowl of popcorn, spilled out the pieces of a puzzle on one of the tables in the middle of the saloon and started one of my favourite movies, 'The Young Victoria', on the screen in front of me. It was absolutely blissful.

One of these days while anchored in a beautiful bay, Thomas sat next to me on the bench in front of the wheelhouse and asked how I was. He could tell I hadn't been doing too well and wanted to talk through it with me. He didn't like seeing me upset.

'What is it you want to do? What are you excited to do here on board?'

'Ummm, I don't know. I guess I still enjoy leading worship and helming, and all the hospitality stuff. And it's pretty beautiful here.'

'OK, so then what are things you *don't* want to do?'

Without hesitation I answered, 'I don't want to be a watch leader.'

I had never said that to anyone though thought it often. I felt inadequate as a watch leader and felt I couldn't handle that kind of responsibility. Plus, I was still filled with anxiety from the previous squall, which really didn't help. But I didn't think I could say that because we were already limited on qualified crew members at that time, so I was needed to fill that spot. And because I don't like to cause any inconvenience to anyone ever, I kept quiet about it.

Thomas just said, 'OK then. You won't be a watch leader for now. We'll work it out. Not a problem.'

I looked back at him with relief in my eyes and gave him a hug. I thanked him for understanding.

I knew though that I would have to step back into that role eventually. We would be having another new team joining us soon and, being one of the few qualified crew members, I was needed. That meant I would have to step back on deck. I couldn't be afraid forever, and I was going to have to face that fear. I was going to have to face that anxiety head-on and overcome it. I would have to step back out on deck.

Right when Thomas said OK, suddenly, without having to carry that responsibility, even for just a short while, I felt in a better position to be able to face that fear. I knew it still wouldn't be easy, but it felt more manageable after that conversation. This is the kind of thing that can happen when you let yourself say how you really feel.

Shortly after our chat on deck, I found a note placed on my pillow.

It was Thomas's beans. His bean warriors.

This is what he said:

'I have gathered a team of beans to care for you in prayer and undercover operations, like pressing the MOB button if you fell overboard and no one saw you.'

Thomas's beans were always the best.

CODE: BEANS ON COVERT OPERATIONS.

SUPERINTENDANT BEAR

0000-0400
1200-1600
WATCH

1600-2000
0400-0800
WATCH

0800-1200
2000-0000
WATCH

Rigging the Mizzen

DATE: February 2014
LOCATION: Kos, Greece
    36° 53' 48.1" N
    27° 17' 17.8" E

Remember that time when we had to untie the mizzen sail from the rigging because the boom had somehow detached itself from the mast? Well, after a lot of repairs and heavy lifting, the boom was securely back in place, so we needed to reattach the repaired sail so we could use it again.

Thomas and I did this on a cool, quiet, late afternoon near sunset while anchored just off the coast of the Greek island, Kos. He had shown me how to do the rope work, which knots to tie, to attach it correctly. So, I harnessed up with coiled rope in hand and scooted my way along the gaff[25] as far astern as I could get. I was sitting up there, nearly hovering over the water about twenty feet below me. I swung my legs down off the gaff to sit on the boom right in between the two so it would be easier to manage.

My job was to attach the sail with the rope through the grommets that lined the head of the sail onto the gaff. It was vitally important to not attach it upside down. As Thomas was working on reattaching the rigging along the mast, I got situated and starting tying.

With the sun setting to my left below the hills of Kos and a rainbow of colour in the sky to my right with nothing but the sea on the horizon, I paused for a moment to take it all in. For

---

25   A strong pole attached to the top of a sail.

that moment, the stress was gone. I could breathe easy. Even if just for a moment. I just had to focus on the task at hand and nothing else mattered.

As I was tying that rope, putting it through the grommet, up around the gaff, and pulling tight, I started to remember how capable I was. That I could accomplish things I had never done before. And also, how awesome my life actually was. It's easy to forget things like that when you're so focused on the things you don't like, the things that are hard.

I didn't realise it then, but that was a glimpse of the redemption I didn't know was on its way. I had been the one who had to take that mizzen sail off in the middle of a storm. I had to secure it to the wheelhouse so it wouldn't blow away into the sea. I was there in its broken state. But I also got to be the one to fix it, to allow it to be used as it was meant to be used again. I got to see its redemption in the sails to come.

Anchor Watches

DATE: *February 2014*
LOCATION: *Greek Islands, South Aegean Sea*
36° 32' 53.2" N
26° 32' 48.2" E

While we were sailing through those Greek Islands for a week or so, we were always anchored in a bay or just off the coast somewhere. We never docked at any port. If we needed to get to land to restock any supplies, we would use the dinghy as a shuttle.

This meant there always needed to be someone on board and especially through the night, someone needed to be on anchor watch. Since we had enough crew at the time, these anchor watches only had to be for one hour per person. While I don't always love having to be awake in the middle of the night for just an hour, I quickly came to love and look forward to those anchor watches. Even ones in the wee hours of the morning, like 02:00.

While my job was to make sure we stayed in relatively the same spot to confirm our anchor was doing its job, it also meant an entire, uninterrupted quiet hour by myself in the wheelhouse. An introvert's delight.

I used these anchor watches to spend some much-needed quiet time with God, with just the sounds of the ship in the background. I had a lot of questions. I was filled with endless doubts and confusion about what I was doing, about who I was. I needed to hear from him. I was tired from feeling his absence on the hard days. For what felt like the first time in a long time, he didn't disappoint. I found he often wouldn't if I actually calmed down enough to listen.

He met me in those dark watches of the night. He reminded me of his truth. He reminded me of his love, his faithfulness. He reminded me of who he was. That he was there. He reminded me of my desire to see and know him but also *his* desire for me to see and know him. Five pages of my journal are filled with the verses and words he spoke to me during those nights.

It was through those anchor watches that God showed me I had to overcome this fear that consumed me. And the only way to do that was to step back out on deck. Even when I was scared. I had to literally step into the fear on deck if I wanted to overcome it.

It was through those anchor watches that God showed me I actually knew the rigging of that boat and how the sails worked and what to do in certain situations so much better than I did before. I wouldn't have learned those things had I not gone through that storm and chose to not give up. I always worried that I didn't know what I was doing half the time when it came to sailing (which was probably true most of the time), and that added to my worry, but I realised that I actually knew a fair amount.

It was through those anchor watches that God showed me I was learning to stay strong and calm through the chaos. The chaos of living on a ship and the chaos of my mind. And somehow, I kept going.

It was through those anchor watches that God reminded me he was a God that could be trusted. Trusted with my life. Trusted through the storms. Trusted with the right now and with my future. Even when I couldn't feel it. And I needed that reminder constantly through all my questioning and doubt that would follow in the weeks and months to come.

There's a tremendous strength and courage that comes from going through a storm. They're certainly not fun. Especially when you feel alone in them. They're always uncomfortable. But when it passes, you can finally see that strength and courage you had all along when you stop to take a breath and look.

Heave To

DATE: February 2014
LOCATION: Mediterranean Sea
$35°\ 16'\ 28.6"\ N$
$29°\ 47'\ 28.5"\ E$

'Let's heave to and have a swim.'

This was my favourite sentence I ever heard Captain Jeremy say.

I will try my best to describe what that means in not-sailor lingo ...

'Heaving to' is the action one would take on a sailboat to stop its forward motion and come to a halt. One way in which this action can be taken is to tack (which means to change course so the wind comes across the other side of the bow) but keep the sail in front (i.e. the jib) tied down with the sheets on the same side of the boat, letting the mainsail move to the other side on its own, and then turn the rudder angle into the wind. In other words, sheeting the headsail to windward. (Makes sense? ... Kind of? ... No?) This resulted in having the sails out over both port and starboard. By doing this, all forward motion stops, and you will pretty much just sit there even though the wind is blowing, filling both sails. How someone figured out that could be a thing, and the fact that it actually is a thing, is beyond me.

'A swim', I think, is pretty self-explanatory, though the means of getting into the water differed from person to person depending on how adventurous they were. From simply climbing slowly down the ladder (which always took at least twice as long to actually get in because it makes you feel how cold the water actually is ...), jumping off the deck, jumping off the very tip of the bowsprit, or rigging up a rope swing off the mainsail boom.

We had several nice, very calm sails around the Greek Islands, which I was so thankful for. I had never seen such calm water before in my life. It was beautiful and a welcome change.

It would be just before lunchtime, and Captain Jeremy would emerge from his cabin to look out at the beautiful day and say, 'Ahh, let's heave to and have a swim, shall we?'

Aye aye, Captain!

We would stop what we were doing, whether on watch, cooking, cleaning, working, reading or even sleeping, and go for a swim. We would enjoy the beautifully clear, blue water, sometimes bringing some shampoo and taking a sea bath (which is harder to do than it sounds ...). Then we'd lie on deck soaking in the sunshine. Lunch would be served outside, and then we'd carry on.

Why did we do that? Well, first of all, it was just fun. A lot of fun. (Except the times when you get a rope burn on your fingers ... that stopped the fun real quick). When you work hard, you need to play hard and also rest hard. We were able to take a break, look out into the open sea where there was no land in sight, switch off for a bit, laugh, have fun and just be. Be fully present where we were. I loved moments like these and was grateful to have them more often. They came from taking a hammock out under the bowsprit, watching the sunrise while completing a maintenance task, and being on anchor watch in the middle of the night. These moments of quiet came when I needed them the most.

It's easy to be constantly going, going, going all the time and never slow down, never stopping to look at where you are, never seeing the beauty around you, never being grateful for the life you have, never just being.

It's easy, at least for my Enneagram One brain, to always be stuck in my head. To be overthinking and overanalysing everything, trying to figure it all out, trying to figure out life when that's an impossible task. Sometimes, I just needed to get out of my head to see the beauty and the good that was all around me always.

It's easy to always be looking at the destination and when you're supposed to get there and that is all you can focus on. That's all you can see: where you're not, yet. But when you heave to and have a swim, for that time, those things don't matter and you can enjoy life, enjoy the water, have lunch and relax. Be fully present where you are.

It makes actually being on the journey even better.

I was always grateful when Captain Jeremy wanted to heave to.

In Paphos

DATE: April 2014
LOCATION: Paphos, Cyprus
   34° 45' 12.6" N
   32° 24' 33.6" E

One of the first things we always did when coming into a new port was the very important task of finding where to buy food. (Anyone else notice how many stories I have about grocery shopping? Interesting how something so mundane and routine can be so memorable ...) After being at sea for several days, you are ready for some fresh fruits and vegetables.

You never know what grocery shopping will be like, but you know it will always be an adventure. You don't know if the store will be close by or far away. Or if they will have a good selection of what you want, if they will speak any English, if you will be able to read any of the signs or labels marking what things are.

When you are shopping for over twenty people for several days' worth of food, you need some good manpower. So, one day in Paphos, I and three others went shopping. Yes, we needed four people for this shopping run. We had a lot of food to get for a new group of people coming on board and a sail to Israel in the near future. So, as was our custom on any shopping trip, we loaded up with the biggest reusable shopping bags we had, as well as our full-size rucksacks. Everything was filled to the brim as we all worked together at checkout to get everything packed and not take forever in line to complete our transaction.

The four of us were weighed down with our ridiculously heavy bags and packs after stocking up, and we had a good twenty-minute walk back to the ship. That twenty minutes was unfortunately extended due to the number of breaks needed to gather up the strength to continue on. My rucksack had carried the weight of the world in milk, flour, butter and meat in the previous months living on the ship. I'm surprised it never had a tear in it, especially on this trip. I felt those gallons of milk on my back during that long walk. I sure got my workout in.

We finally made it, all incredibly tired, and dropped the bags on the quayside, careful to not drop the bag with the eggs down too hard. Those eggs were precious to us for Saturday Breakfast.

What I haven't yet mentioned about this particular situation was our very unique way of getting onto the ship in this port in Paphos. Now, under normal circumstances, we had a long gangway that would bridge the gap between the ship and the quayside. Easy and extremely effective. This day would not have the same effectiveness.

Let me back up for a second.

When we arrived at Paphos, the dock we were to be moored stern to was along the back end of the marina. We were one of the biggest ships in port, so there weren't many options for us to go where we would fit. When we started backing into our spot (done by the exceptional driving skills of Captain Jeremy), we discovered the water was too shallow for us to be moored fully astern like we had hoped. We risked hitting our rudder to land which would have been a bad thing. We had to stop just before by watching our depth measurements carefully. We went as far back as we could, but our gangway wouldn't be able to bridge that gap. Some other way of getting off needed to be figured out.

Being the ingenious sailors they were, several crew members came up with a pretty brilliant idea. I only found out the details of this plan when I came up on deck to see one of our biggest fenders attached to the end of the gangway and Captain Jeremy, with the help of a few others, literally throwing the entire gangway overboard on the port side. All I heard was a huge splash as I looked on in confusion, watching our gangway disappear over the rail.

'What the heck are you guys doing?'

I hadn't seen it was attached to the railing, I honestly thought they were just throwing it overboard, and I was concerned.

I looked over the rail to see the gangway acting as a ladder with the fender pushing against our other biggest fender (which they had already thrown over) along the side of the ship in the water. These two fenders next to each other brought the gangway out enough to be able to easily walk up and down it. I looked up with a smile on my face at how ridiculous yet incredibly smart that move was. They then continued with their plan and drove the dinghy over, which we had lowered before backing in.

The next step was to make a pulley system for the dinghy with which we could use to go back and forth from the end of the gangway in the water to shore. With blocks in place onshore, connected to the dinghy and back to the gangway, our system was set. We had to pull ourselves back and forth while sitting in the dinghy to get from one side to the other.

Again, the situations I often found myself in …

On any normal day, it was a decent amount of work to pull yourself over, but on a day like the day we had four people with arms and backs full of groceries, it was a whole other experience.

We loaded up the dinghy as much as we could with all the food from our shopping trip. The dinghy was definitely riding low in the water from its weight. I grasped the rope as firmly as I could and pulled with all my might until there was movement across the water towards our destination.

As part of everyday life on Next Wave, all things paused when groceries arrived, and a grocery chain was then formed. This was a line of people going from outside, down the stairs, and into the galley. It was oddly one of the things I loved from that first trip to Tesco in Liverpool and made me happy every time.

I had called several people up, and we began to unload the groceries from the dinghy, passing them up the bobbing gangway and down into the galley. Remember, those bags were incredibly heavy. So, after a good workout of walking back with it all strapped to my back and in my arms, I then had to lift it all up from the dinghy to the person standing just above me. Because of the weight of it, it pushed the fenders hard against each other and the bottom step or two of the gangway was submerged in water, so I had to be careful where I stood if I didn't want to have wet feet.

After several trips of this to get everything on board, the task was completed and some much-needed stretching commenced.

MOB

DATE: April 2014
LOCATION: Sail – Paphos, Cyprus to Herzliya, Israel
34° 29' 46.8" N
32° 28' 1.7" E

Sailing from Cyprus to Israel was quite an exciting one. Due in part probably to having a film crew on board at the time, so we did a lot of fun stuff to give them a full picture of what it was like to sail and allow them ample footage.

We had set off after a long morning of trying to work out all the paperwork for us to leave (happened often if you hadn't noticed ...), and once we were underway with the mainsail up, I went to take a nap before it was my turn to be on watch. I became exceptionally good at figuring out the best schedule that worked for me for when I napped, ate, and was on watch depending on what time my watches were. My disciplined regimen. I knew that if I took any seasick tablets and didn't get a nap in right after, I became the most apathetic, annoyed and stubborn person ever. I remember the first time this happened when I first took a seasick tablet: I was sitting in front of the wheelhouse, and everyone was on deck getting ready to raise some sails. I was asked excitedly if I wanted to help, and I just sat there with my arms folded and said, 'nope', not even looking up at them. It was a strange side effect that I did everything I could to avoid after that first time.

I was taking my scheduled nap when the general alarm sounded. That's always the best way to wake up: with the loudest, most annoying bell ringing constantly right outside your cabin and you have to immediately spring into action. I raced up to the wheelhouse to ask Captain Jeremy what was going on, and he said it was a man overboard drill. I looked out to see everyone lining the deck with their arms outstretched pointing towards where this 'man' was. In this particular drill, it was a fender that had been thrown overboard that we needed to retrieve. (Best not to throw an actual person overboard for practice if it wasn't necessary.) That was the first step when anyone yelled, 'Man overboard!' Everyone was to stop whatever they were doing to look and constantly point to where they spotted that person to keep eyes on them and not lose them to the swell. This drill was a required practice when sailing in the unfortunate event of someone actually falling overboard while out at sea. Thankfully, I never had to do this for real.

As crew, we all had positions assigned to us for every kind of emergency situation. I knew my job for every emergency drill we had to perform. So, when I found out it was a man overboard drill, I knew immediately where I was to go. My assigned position was in the aft to lower the dinghy into the water so the people being lowered could go out and rescue our man.

I took my position, barefoot because I had just jumped out of bed (and I didn't often wear shoes while sailing as long as the weather was good), and Thomas walked back to get ready to take his position in the driver's seat of the dinghy. He was suited up with a life jacket and radio in his hand, and I was ready to lead the lowering operations to get him down in the water safely.

He immediately walked up beside me and asked, 'Kellie, where's your life jacket? Go get it on.'

Umm, what?

The crew member whose assigned position for this drill was to be the second man in the dinghy wasn't actually with us, so I was supposed to be next in line to fill that spot. I knew it worked like that with our emergency positions, but I was so in the zone of just remembering my assigned job that it didn't cross my mind that we were missing someone. With a bit of confusion, I silently turned around to grab a life jacket from the wheelhouse. I suited up for an unknown adventure. I was kind of winging it, with Thomas's instruction.

We were hove to in relatively choppy water when Thomas and I had climbed into the dinghy and were being lowered to the waterline. He revved the engine as we splashed down into the sea and detached ourselves. We were off to find our fender. With the help of everyone on deck pointing, I could see the fender off in the distance, so I gave the direction to Thomas, and we raced towards it. It was a wild ride through those choppy waves, our front-end riding high in the air. I might have gotten airborne a few times. Racing out through the water in that dinghy, I felt like the coolest person ever.

We reached the fender, and I pulled it in to safety. Next, I radioed to Captain Jeremy that we retrieved our man and would be heading back. He informed us to come alongside the starboard side. Relaying that to Thomas, he revved again through the choppy waters to race back.

When we made it back alongside, I thought the job was done. As was common, I thought wrong.

The next thing I knew, I heard someone in a bright orange life jacket splash in the water behind me, and we had to rescue her. We pulled her up into the dinghy and practiced using the Jason's Cradle. Why it is called that, I have no idea. But it's a very interesting contraption that attaches to the ship and the person needing a rescue lies inside of it, and it literally rolls them up on deck.

She made it up safely, so I turned to face Thomas and initiated a well-deserved high five. What a great team we were.

Once she was up, my job on the water was finally done and then I had to be on the raising party to get the dinghy back on board in its proper place. It had been a little bit of a rough lowering process earlier, so he wanted it to be done well this time when we brought him back up. When I had climbed back up on deck, Thomas yelled up to me and said, 'Kellie, impress me.'

I think I impressed him.

For having very little idea what my role was throughout this drill, I did a pretty good job. Mostly because Thomas was really good at guiding me through it all. I just never managed to get back to my nap after all this excitement. It was my turn to be on watch by the time the drills were finished.

After all was said and done, I had a moment of asking myself, *What is my life that I get to do this?*

My job that day consisted of being woken up from a nap by an alarm to jump into emergency drills involving a wild ride in the dinghy, followed by an extensive fire drill, then being on watch in the middle of the night in the middle of the Mediterranean Sea teaching people about sailing. These are the kinds of stories I can't make up. The kinds of stories I look back on and think how absolutely crazy it sounds now. The kinds of stories that happened during a really tough time in my life, where I felt so uncomfortable and so far away from God and so frustrated by him, but yet he was still writing awesome stories for me to live every day.

My perceived experience of his absence made no difference to him.

He was still there. And still had really good things ahead that I couldn't see.

Jerusalem

DATE: April 2014
LOCATION: Jerusalem, Israel
   31° 46' 38.1" N
   35° 13' 41.9" E

Sailing into Israel was an experience. We had a Discipleship Bible School with us on board by this point. It was one of those where we sailed to the places they were studying in the Bible. So, of course, Israel had to be on that list of destinations. Israel is kind of a big deal in the Bible.

With our destination in sight on the horizon, so was a fully loaded boat out in front of us. And by fully loaded, I mean guns. A boat with heavy artillery and armed men were racing towards us. They circled us several times and escorted us into the entrance of the Herzliya Marina. The deck grew eerily quiet.

Herzliya is a fancy marina. There were some gorgeous and very expensive pleasure yachts lining each dock. And we were to be berthed right in the middle of two of the fanciest.

Captain Jeremy is by far the best I've seen at manoeuvring Next Wave. Watching him navigate his way into tight spots was beyond impressive. And it had to be when tasked with coming in between those two yachts. I stood at the stern watching for only as long as I could handle due to being so nervous. The others on the yachts on either side of us were equally, if not exponentially more nervous. I watched them put out more and more fenders on the side of their yachts than there were before we got there. Somehow, Captain Jeremy brought us in backward perfectly in the middle with only a couple metres distance between us and those next to us on each side. It still baffles me how he did this.

That fully loaded boat was still hanging around through all of this. So, when we were safely secured, Israeli police boarded with their dogs to search the ship and question us. In the intense sun and heat of the day, we all had to sit on deck while they searched. (It still surprises me that those dogs didn't find the small container of gun powder someone in the aft cabin may or may not have had to use for his handmade, fully functional mini cannons ...). After questioning a handful of us, they took us all to the immigration office on the other side of the marina to get our visas for our stay. They gave us an official piece of paper with a stamp to put in our passports. Had they stamped our actual passports, there were a few countries we would have been denied entrance to just for the simple reason that we had been to Israel. Definitely an interesting introduction to a very different climate and culture of a place.

After all that excitement, we could get on with our usual day-to-day.

―――――⇜⇜―――――

During the week we were in Israel, the Bible school had been out every day walking, touring, studying and seeing the sights of a country with an incredible history. I had to stay back on the ship most of that week, but there was one day when I and three others took the opportunity to see the city of Jerusalem. We were so close, so we had to make it happen.

We set off in the morning to head to the bus stop. After waiting there for longer than I felt we should have, we just grabbed a taxi instead to take us to the bus station in Tel Aviv. It was from there we could take a bus to the heart of Jerusalem. And what a beautiful bus ride it was. It took us up, around, and through the beautiful mountains of that amazing country. We all kept looking around at each other at how crazy it was that we were actually on our way to freaking Jerusalem.

We reached Jerusalem and began our quest to find the Old City. Having no idea where it was, we asked around and thankfully just had to head straight down the street we were already on. So, we walked. To our right, we saw a little market and decided to take a quick detour and check out the local goods. There were stalls filled with freshly baked bread, crisp fruits and vegetables, olives in jars (not for me ...), spices in buckets, clothes, and nuts (also not for me ...). We took our time walking this street among locals and tourists alike, attempting to understand the signs in another language with prices and symbols that made no sense to me. There is quite a difference between a dollar and a shekel.

Continuing on, we saw the walls to the Old City in front of us. We went through the Jaffa Gate and into the heart of the Old City bazaar. It's like a labyrinth in there. With every turn, the thought that Jesus walked through these streets kept coming to mind.

These streets led us to the Church of the Holy Sepulchre. This was the place thought to be where Jesus was crucified, buried, and where he rose again. This church was beautifully decorated in every corner. We ascended the stairs to the place where Jesus would have been crucified. Here, underneath a sheet of glass, was the rock of Calvary that was said to have the hole where the cross was planted into the ground. If seeing all that doesn't bring the Bible to life, I don't know what does.

Our next journey led us to the Wailing Wall. We watched from a distance as people approached the wall.

After our morning of walking, we sat under a tree on a stone wall, hot and hungry, to enjoy our peanut butter and jelly sandwiches to decide what to do next. One of my travel buddies was determined to swim in the Dead Sea. And I really appreciated that determination. She managed to find a taxi driver who agreed to drive us there, which was about an hour away. And not only that, but he agreed to wait for us while we swam and then drive us back. We pondered on it for a bit, deciding if we wanted to spend the money for this adventure (an amount that was actually quite reasonable for what we were asking). We concluded that this was truly a once-in-a-lifetime kind of thing and that it would be worth it. We'd regret being so close to the Dead Sea and not seeing it and swimming in it.

We piled into the taxi to set out through the desert to the lowest point on earth. Our driver turned tour guide first took us up to the Mount of Olives. This place is also kind of a big deal. It's where Jesus travelled through when he first entered Jerusalem on a donkey (Matt. 21), where he prayed for God to take the cup from him, and where he was betrayed by Judas (Matt. 26).

Leaving the Mount of Olives that overlooked the Old City, we drove off to the Dead Sea. On our drive through the hill-laden desert, I thought about how the people of the Bible had to walk through that kind of terrain to get to Jerusalem. The Bible is full of the Israelites walking, and now I could catch even just a glimpse of the conditions they walked through, blown away that their sandals never wore out (Deut. 29:5).

I have had my fair share of gorgeous drives through the mountains of Colorado. I always loved watching for the signs stating what elevation I was at and watching it climb. My favourite had always been going through Vail Pass to see the elevation at nearly 11,000 feet. On this drive through the desert in Israel, I watched for elevation signs. But this time it was very different. They were all negative numbers. This was hard to comprehend. We were about to be 1,400 feet below sea level. That didn't even seem possible.

Descending even further down to the sea from where our driver dropped us off, I saw a sign that explained best practices for getting into the Dead Sea. It apparently wasn't the kind you just walked into, let alone jumped. I looked out at the number of other people with the same idea as us, and they were all just floating. It still didn't feel real, didn't feel like that was actually possible even though I was seeing it. As per instructions, I had to wade out into the water, squat down and simply lean back. But what happened when I leaned back was an unusual experience. My legs bounced unwillingly out in front of me, my toes popping out of the water with ease. The Dead Sea is not a sea you swim in. It's a sea you float in. Still one of the weirdest experiences of my life. Like all those around me, I floated with no effort of my own. And when I tried to keep my legs down beneath me, they would flop back up behind me.

One word of caution for those ever wanting to experience the waters of the Dead Sea – don't get the water in your eyes. Or anywhere around your mouth. It's pretty awful. Be careful when your legs flop up behind you.

After floating for a while, we rinsed off as much salt as we could from what had accumulated on our bodies and in our hair (feeling extremely exfoliated) and went to find our taxi man who was patiently waiting for us on a bench. He asked us if we wanted to take a little detour and see the city of Jericho. We were already loving this adventure, so we agreed. He also told us he would take us free of charge because it was where he was from, and he was very proud of that.

Jericho is another place of incredible biblical significance. But the one that got me that day was when we passed by a certain sycamore tree. This sycamore tree was supposedly the same one that Zacchaeus climbed up so he could see Jesus walking by in Luke 19. It was a story I was so familiar with that to be seeing it, even if it wasn't the exact tree or the exact place, made that story come to life. I was standing in the street that was once filled with people who just wanted a glimpse of Jesus. A place that one man was so desperate for that glimpse that he climbed a tree, and Jesus noticed and wanted to go to his place for dinner that night.

Not wanting the journey to end and wanting to see more, I knew we needed to start heading back to get home to the ship before too late. Our tour guide got us back to the city; we thanked him immensely for the sights he allowed us to see, and we hopped on a bus back to Tel Aviv. Being out of cash by our last taxi ride, we finally made it home after a pretty incredible day.

To have gotten to be in such a place rich in history and significance, to walk the streets Jesus walked, to see where he died on a cross, to see the terrain the Israelites traversed, and to swim in the Dead Sea is a day I'll not soon forget. And one I'm incredibly grateful to have been given.

Outside Watch

DATE: April 2014
LOCATION: Sail – Herzliya, Israel to Mersin, Turkey
    34° 42' 23.8" N
    34° 50' 33.5" E

To be honest, I don't remember much of our sail from Israel to Turkey. Sometimes, all those nautical miles just blend together, and I can't distinguish between sails. But sometimes I can. But this time, I can't. And that's OK.

At this point, I had started being a watch leader again. After our Greek island-hopping sails, I was able to gather the courage to step back into that role and face my fears, which were thankfully diminishing. It helped that Captain Jeremy was a great support. Feeling better-equipped and ready to take that responsibility back, I was able to walk in that role with more confidence.

It was a relatively smooth sail, I think. And, if I'm remembering the right sail which, again, I could be mixing up with another one, I got to sail by the stars.

I love stars. You should know this by now. There was one night when it was so calm and so clear. I had gone outside to see what the weather and sea state was, and when I came back inside, I said to the rest of my watch team, 'So, we're going to have watch outside tonight.' We spent the entire night watch outside (with the occasional check inside to plot our position and make sure we were actually staying on course because I was a good watch leader like that). I loved that we had another helm outside on deck to make this night possible.

I didn't sail by the stars like the sailors of old did by plotting where the stars were and using one of those fancy contraptions known as a sextant and doing all that math. But I used the compass to point us in the right direction for where we wanted to go, and once I was on course, I looked up to find a few stars I could use as reference points for a while. When I could find a good, bright, easily recognised star or cluster, I would see where it was in relation to something on the ship like the mast or a shroud[26], and steer to keep it in place.

Helming by sight and the stars was just the best and getting to spend the night doing that on deck with some pretty great people was pretty great.

What I actually do remember from this particular sail was that the next morning, we were looking out across the land of Turkey and had no idea where we were supposed to be going. It was such a new marina that it wasn't on any of our charts or maps. We had to rely on just the GPS coordinates were given and binoculars to find it.

But don't worry. We found it.

---

[26] Part of the rigging that held the mast up.

Bike Adventures

DATE: April 2014
LOCATION: Mersin, Turkey
  36° 46' 11.2" N
  34° 33' 57.4" E

My friend, Tessa, and I liked to go on adventures together. We had our first adventure on a couple bikes exploring the beautiful fields of Cyprus. Then again when Captain Jeremy decided to heave to and have a swim. One day, to be safe, Captain Jeremy had asked that the dinghy be lowered into the water in case of emergency. I answered that direct order with a question.

'Umm, since it's already going to be in the water, would it be alright if I took it out for a test drive? You know, I just really need to get some more good practice in with driving that thing.' My humble attempt at showing how responsible I was ...

'Sure, that sounds alright.'

With a big smile on my face, I grabbed Tessa and we hopped in the dinghy for a spin. We circled the ship a few times, taking photos, enjoying the view, the weather, and the company. It sure was good (and necessary ...) practice.

When we arrived in Turkey, Tessa and I decided that we should go for another bike ride together. We decided to go on our day off, but that day, it happened to be raining. A lot.

We went anyways.

We weaved along a gorgeous path with the coast on our left and the city buzzing around on our right. After getting completely soaked in the rain, we took a turn down some semi-busy streets. We came to a gathering of sorts which kind of looked like a little market with different stalls of food and picnic tables (all covered because, well ... it was raining). We dismounted, out of respect of course, and walked ourselves and our bikes around it. I have never felt so out of place in my life. There I was, a blonde, American girl soaked by the rain in a bright green hooded jacket walking around Turkish natives in their traditional Turkish dress with another blonde Dutch girl looking the same as me.

We didn't stick around long and continued our journey around the city of Mersin.

Tessa is from the Netherlands. They bike there a lot. So, she had no fear on a bike in the middle of the road or in crowded places. Even if that bike had no brakes. Which hers, unfortunately, did not.

After exploring the city a bit, we made our way back to the ship, heading towards the coast. That's the nice thing about living on a ship in a marina. If you get lost, look for water and you'll be able to find the boat again. We made it back to the main road, so all that was left to do was get to the other side. However, there wasn't much of a crosswalk. We just decided to risk it and go across at a random spot when we could find a break in the traffic. When we spotted the break, I went first and was able to easily cross, popping my front bike tire up the curb.

Tessa was following closely behind when I suddenly heard her yell, 'I have no brakes!'

I looked back just in time to see her crash right into the curb, nearly flying over the handlebars. She had enough control to stop herself, but all I could do, like a good friend, was laugh. And before you think me insensitive, she was also laughing a whole lot, probably more than me. She slowly walked the injured bike over to where I was through fits of laughter. We were just two soaking wet out-of-towners, crashing bikes on curbs and jaywalking. We took a minute to compose ourselves so we could assess the damage. Thankfully, it was just the chain that had come out of place, so it was an easy fix. (I didn't know it then, but this kind of foreshadowed another adventure Tessa and I would have months later when I might have crashed into a parked car while driving a moped …)

With the laughter dying down just a little bit, though still with massive smiles on our wet faces from the rain, we continued on back along the path to the ship.

A few days before this, we discovered that the supermarket nearest to us was selling strawberries at about two Lira per kilo, that's about $0.50 per pound. That's a cheap price for that amount of strawberries.

As Tessa and I were on our way back to the ship, we passed by this store and decided to get some strawberries to reward ourselves for the adventure and near-death experience we just had and to have a snack for the movie we were planning to watch when we got back. So, she stayed outside with the bikes as I went in, dripping wet, to get a big box of strawberries.

With strawberries purchased, we concluded our journey, dried off, put on warm clothes, probably made some popcorn, and enjoyed a movie with a box of strawberries.

A good way to spend a day off.

Turkey – England

DATE: April 2014
LOCATION: Mersin, Turkey
      36° 46' 11.2" N
      34° 33' 57.4" E

It was 04:00 in a small marina in Mersin, Turkey, just outside of Tarsus, my guitar case full of more than just a guitar, and a backpack strapped to my back. It was time to take my long-awaited break to England. I had been on the ship for nearly 9 months straight so I was looking forward to a change in scenery. It would be a journey to get there though. It would take two days to cross half the length of Turkey (it's a big country) and then a long flight over Europe to get there. It's the kind of journey your mom freaks out about until you've made it.

    I packed in the car with Captain Jeremy and two of his friends and we embarked in darkness on a nine-hour drive along the coast and through the mountains of Turkey, our road becoming curvier as the sun slowly began to rise behind us. A stretch break showed us the beginnings of some pretty amazing sights we were going to see along the way.

    About four hours or so into the journey, we decided it was time for breakfast. We stumbled upon a small restaurant at the top of the coastline overlooking the sea and enjoyed the most amazing Turkish breakfast I've ever had. Well, it's the only traditional Turkish breakfast I've ever had, but it was seriously the best. We had scrambled eggs and sausage with the most perfect blend of spices, there were vegetables, fresh bread, homemade honey, apricots, and dates.

We continued on our journey, happily full, trading seats around every once in a while to get a different view from the car, counting all the mosques I saw along the way, until we made it to Antalya, almost 300 miles away from our starting point. After exploring the city for a bit, I had to go meet up with the person who would take me to the place I would be staying for the night. It was one of those friend-of-a-friend-of-a-friend kind of situations. She took good care of me, and I had a bed for the night and breakfast in the morning in a random city in Turkey that I had never been to before with someone I had only just met.

The next morning, I was walked to a bus stop where I got on a bus that took me all around the city before going to another, bigger bus station. I then immediately got on another bus which would take me the four hours to the Dalaman airport. But this was unlike any bus I had ever been on. First of all, it was driving through Turkey, so that was a beautiful new experience, but every seat had its own television screen, and a guy was serving complimentary refreshments up and down the aisle like on an airplane. Quality bus service right there.

We came to a rest stop halfway through, and I decided it would probably be a good idea to take advantage of the toilet break. However, I didn't find a toilet, but rather a hole in the ground. Awesome. Squatty Potty. It's always good to experience other cultures, right?

I made it to Dalaman, and it's a good thing I was paying attention since the driver didn't announce at all where we were, and he had just been letting people off at random stops whenever they asked. I'm pretty sure he let a guy off in the middle of the highway in the middle of nowhere at one point. After learning how this bus driver did things, I watched the signs on the road a bit closer. I'm incredibly thankful I pay attention to detail, especially when travelling, and that I am physically incapable of falling asleep on public transportation. And for good reason. I saw signs for Dalaman and had to yell at the driver that I wanted to get off. I'm not sure if he entirely understood the words I said, but he got the message. Had I not spoken up, I'm pretty sure he would have just kept driving and I would have been lost in Turkey.

My next task was to find a taxi to take me to the airport. Slight problem though: I had a very limited amount of Turkish Lira left in my wallet (I had splurged on those strawberries ...). Despite that, this nice taxi man agreed to take what I could give him and get me to the airport, though I doubt it was worth his effort. But I'm grateful for his generosity (or maybe it was boredom ... it felt like we were just out in the desert somewhere).

I arrived at the airport a whole seven hours before my flight was due to depart. The international terminal was completely empty. But I was OK with it. The fact that I had finally made it to this destination and no longer had to navigate my way through a foreign country was a relief to me. So, I went to sit at a café that happened to be open in the parking lot. I sat there for the next few hours, occasionally watching a group of passengers coming down meeting their tour buses and taxis while drawing endless colourful circles in my notebook to pass the time.

Finally, it was time to check in with the masses and board my flight to England. But not before finding a sign in the bathroom that told me I wasn't allowed to wash my feet in the sink. Interesting warning sign. That only means that someone did it once, and it probably wasn't pleasant.

We took off, and a few hours later, I landed in England with a sigh of relief and contentment, even though it was 01:00 and I was very tired. As I stepped outside the plane to walk down the stairs to a bus that would take me to the terminal, I was met by the glorious English weather I had missed so much – overcast, cold and wet. Happiness abounded. The kind of happiness you feel when you come home.

Note to self: next time, maybe just pay a little extra for a flight at a closer airport ... but then again, where's the fun in that?

Where Were You?

DATE: *May 2014*
LOCATION: *Harpenden, England*
51° 49' 32.1" N
0° 21' 35.9" W

I was picked up in the middle of the night at the airport by one of my favourite people who said she didn't do this kind of thing for just anyone. I felt loved and welcomed. I felt like I was back home. I was finally back in England, one of my favourite places.

I was so ready to use that time to really process life. To finally rest, go for runs through my favourite fields, have a pint at a favourite pub, see some of my favourite people. It wasn't perfect and I had some tough conversations as I was trying to figure out where my head and heart were at with the whole continuing to work and live on Next Wave. But it was good. So good. So needed.

I had some intense debrief times with someone I deeply respected to really get to the root of the fear, anger and anxiety I had been experiencing for quite some time. We began to pray about the storms. Well, one storm in particular. You know the one I'm talking about. That stupid squall. The one where I felt like God had abandoned me. The one that grew this anxiety inside me that came to the surface whenever the winds picked up. The anxiety that crippled me. I would feel it, go find Captain Jeremy in the wheelhouse and tell him I needed a minute. I'd sit on the couch in the Nav Office until I could calm down.

I finally asked God, 'Where were you in that storm?'

Being back in England made me realise how uncomfortable I had been for a long time, how low I had gotten, how tired I was. Despite moments of joy and amazing, once-in-a-lifetime experiences sprinkled throughout, I still felt empty and pretty hopeless.

It had been a season of feeling God's absence, and I didn't love it. Despite that, it was somehow a season he had invited me into. Though I couldn't understand why.

When Jesus was baptised, God opened up the heavens and told everyone around that he loved Jesus, that Jesus was his son, that he was well pleased with Jesus (Matt. 3:16–17). Then, God invited Jesus into the desert (Matt. 4:1). He invited Jesus to be hungry and thirsty, to be tired, to be tempted by the devil. To be alone.

I'm sure Jesus probably didn't enjoy those forty days and nights in the desert. But God invited Jesus to be uncomfortable for a bit, to feel his absence for a bit. But with every temptation from the devil, Jesus held onto the truth of who God was and what he'd spoken.

He knew in his gut what was true, as uncomfortable as he was. He made that choice. He could have easily given into that temptation and been angry with God for allowing him to go through that. But he made the choice to trust in what he knew to be true. Trust in this all-knowing, all-loving God. Even when it didn't make sense.

I was picturing that moment in the storm, that moment of feeling helpless and abandoned, that moment sitting on top of the wheelhouse with a fear I had never known before. I couldn't understand how a loving God could have put me through that.

I asked again, 'Where were you in that storm?' and then the picture changed. It zoomed out to a bird's eye view of the ship from behind, and I saw God's hands surrounding the boat.

He was there the whole time. He was carrying us through. He was with us. He was taking care of us. Things could have been so much worse during that storm, but his hands surrounded us the whole time, protecting us. I just couldn't see it in the moment.

But he was with me.

And once again, my perceived experience of his absence made no difference to him.

I knew that the ship was where God wanted me to be, no matter how much I wanted to go home. My gut was telling me to stay, and nine times out of ten, my gut is right. It's a very reliable gut.

But I had to start making the choice every day to be there. Making the choice every day to trust that it was where God had me, that there was a purpose in it. Making the choice every day to trust in this all-knowing, all-loving God. Trust that he was there and that he was good even when it didn't feel like it.

End on a Good One

DATE: December 2013
LOCATION: Gozo
   36° 1' 38.5" N
   14° 18' 16.4" E

During this time in England, I was wrestling. Wrestling with where I had been, with where I was and with where I was going. Wrestling with everything that happened and everything that didn't happen. I was a mess. It all felt to be too much and not enough at the same time. I wanted to be sure of what I would do next so the time in England helped tremendously with allowing myself the space to figure it out. At least as much as I could (which wasn't much). I was trying to decide if I should stay on the ship and finish out my commitment or move on sooner than originally planned.

There is a gorgeous pathway that goes for miles through the countryside near YWAM Harpenden called The Nickey Line. There's a stairway that leads down to this beloved path right outside the entrance of The Oval. It's a former railway line which linked some of the smaller town nearby turned public footpath. And it's my favourite. Like, I get emotional thinking about it because of how much I love it. When I lived on the Oval, I would go down those stairs to The Nickey Line quite literally every day and go on adventures through the fields. I came to know that line so well that one day I made a map of my favourite loop so someone else could experience its greatness. It became my place to go on walks and runs and process life and enjoy its beauty. Anytime I got the chance to be near it, I took it.

So, I took a walk along the Nickey Line. I remembered back to something that happened when we were still in Gozo six months before. It was a conversation I had with God which settled deep in my gut.

I would often need to find moments to get away, to get outside, to get out of my head. The way I found to do this was through my many walks along the water's edge on the island of Gozo. This walk overlooked Mgarr Marina on the right, the island of Comino on the left, and Malta in the distance just ahead. It was here that I was alone – and usually no one walked by, so I could talk (sometimes loudly) to God.

During this particular conversation, I was at what I thought was the end of my rope, and I didn't want to be on the ship anymore. (Little did I know what was to come, this was before the squall ...). But I knew that it was where God wanted me to be. So, I asked him a question.

I asked, 'How long do you want me on the ship for? I know if I have an end date, I would be able to make the most of my time here. So how long?'

'Until the end of the next DTS.'

I wasn't particularly thrilled by that answer though. That end was over a year out.

I somehow felt though that he didn't just want me *around* for the next DTS but he wanted me to *lead* the next DTS. For the previous few years, I had many words spoken and given to me about leadership, about how God wanted to raise me up as a leader. One such word also included that maybe God was leading me towards leading a school, a DTS to be specific. I didn't like it at the time because I felt inadequate (a feeling I've had to overcome quite a lot in my life), but I remembered that word and knew what God wanted me to do.

'Umm, can I ask why though?'

I wasn't at my best in that moment, and I couldn't understand how or why God wanted to use me in that way. He wanted me to lead and disciple a group of people on a boat sailing in the Mediterranean Sea. It didn't make sense to me. I didn't get it. I didn't feel like I was capable of that.

But his answer surprised me.

His answer stuck with me and was something I held on tight to. His answer was what I kept coming back to every time I doubted what in the world I was doing living on a boat.

'Because I want you to end on a good one.'

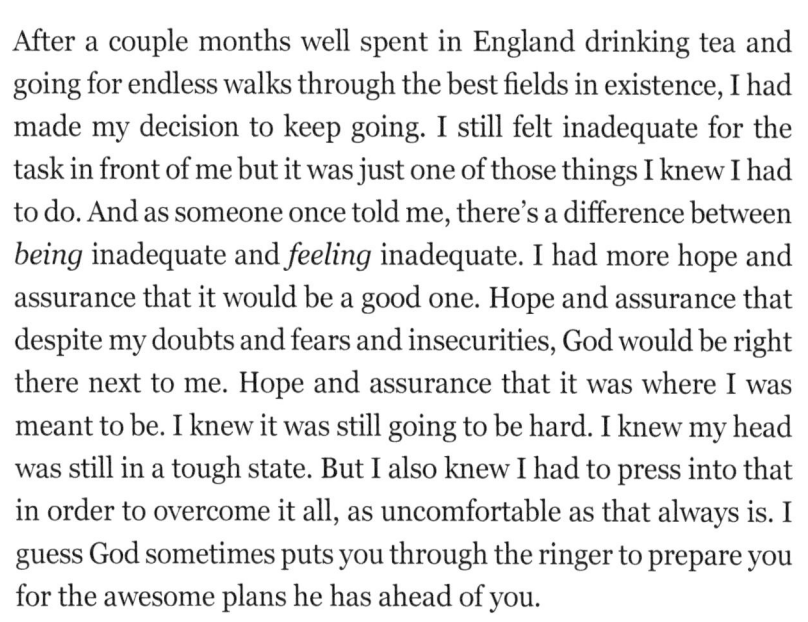

After a couple months well spent in England drinking tea and going for endless walks through the best fields in existence, I had made my decision to keep going. I still felt inadequate for the task in front of me but it was just one of those things I knew I had to do. And as someone once told me, there's a difference between *being* inadequate and *feeling* inadequate. I had more hope and assurance that it would be a good one. Hope and assurance that despite my doubts and fears and insecurities, God would be right there next to me. Hope and assurance that it was where I was meant to be. I knew it was still going to be hard. I knew my head was still in a tough state. But I also knew I had to press into that in order to overcome it all, as uncomfortable as that always is. I guess God sometimes puts you through the ringer to prepare you for the awesome plans he has ahead of you.

So, with my bags packed again, I headed back to Gozo, ready to jump in and make the most of it no matter what came my way.

Part 4
TO HIS REDEMPTION

October 2014 – December 2014

Gozo, Malta – Sciacca, Sicily: 3 days, 135 nm
Sciacca, Sicily – Palermo, Sicily: 2 days, 119 nm
Palermo, Sicily – Cefalù – Termini – Cefalù, Sicily: 3 days, 29 nm
Cefalù, Sicily – Messina, Sicily: 2 days, 92 nm
Messina, Sicily – Catania, Sicily: 2 days, 52 nm
Catania, Sicily – Syracuse, Sicily: 3 days, 52 nm
Syracuse, Sicily – Gozo, Malta: 3 days, 62 nm

Others went out on the sea in ships;
they were merchants on the mighty waters.
They saw the works of the Lord,
his wonderful deeds in the deep.
For he spoke and stirred up a tempest
that lifted high the waves.
They mounted up to the heavens
and went down to the depths;
in their peril, their courage melted away.
They reeled and staggered like drunken men;
they were at their wits' end.
Then they cried out to the Lord in their trouble,
and he brought them out of their distress.
He stilled the storm to a whisper;
the waves of the sea were hushed.
They were glad when it grew calm,
and he guided them to their desired haven.
Let them give thanks to the Lord for his unfailing love
and his wonderful deeds for mankind.
Let them exalt him in the assembly of the people
and praise him in the council of the elders.
Psalm 107:23–32

Back in Gozo

DATE: July 2014
LOCATION: Qala, Gozo
36° 2' 7.8" N
14° 19' 9.1" E

I don't do well with heat. Especially when that heat is accompanied by humidity. It makes me mad. Pretty much the moment I step outside into those kinds of conditions, I'm just immediately pissed. It's hot in Gozo during the summer. It is, in fact, a Mediterranean island after all. I avoided going outside as much as possible unless I absolutely had to. It was this summer when I truly understood the value and brilliance of why hot countries adopt siesta as a regular thing. It honestly makes so much sense. Most days, I was perfectly content sitting on the couch with a fan blowing cool air directly on my face. Other days, though, I wanted to be outside but hated the heat, so it was an irritating dilemma.

For about a month or so, I had the amazing opportunity of living in a beautiful villa on the small island of Gozo. Definitely not something I would have ever envisioned being able to say. My days were spent writing stories, exploring the island and preparing for the upcoming DTS I would be leading.

During those hot summer months, I lived by these words: *If you can't handle the heat, just go swimming.* I did a lot of swimming that month. I swam in the small pool at the villa quite literally every day. Occasionally, if we were up for it, we would head to Hondoq Bay (another Maltese word I'll try to help you pronounce - hawn - dock), just a short drive down a very steep hill. We would often walk over to this small cove away from the crowd and jump into the refreshing sea. A few times, we brought our snorkel gear. One day, I spent three glorious hours in the water looking out for hermit crabs, sea centipedes and little fishes and flipping and spinning through the water.

I found swimming in the Med to be significantly easier than swimming anywhere else. The water was salty which added a bit of buoyancy which I needed to help me stay afloat (thankfully not as much buoyancy as the Dead Sea provided, but you couldn't really swim in that particular sea anyways ...).

One morning during my stay at the villa, I woke up, had some delicious granola for breakfast and decided to go on a walk to explore where I would be living for the next several weeks. Exploring new places on foot had kind of become my thing, and I quite enjoyed it. While I knew it was going to be hot, I mentally prepared myself for that before I set out. I didn't want to start the day pissed.

Gozo has hills. A lot of them. They're everywhere. My morning walk began by going up a very large hill. No surprise there. After walking up the hill and along the road for a while, passing by horse stables, I found a path of sorts which would begin a descent. Before embarking down that path, I needed to decide whether or not I actually wanted to descend knowing that eventually, I would have to walk back up. It was hot (have I said that too many times?) and would continue to get hotter as the day went on and the sun rose higher in the sky. I figured it was early enough in the day that I had time for such an adventure. And if I made it down to the water, I could jump in for a moment to cool off if I needed. That was the only incentive I needed to carry on.

This decision proved to be the right one. I waded through the refreshing water at the base of the hill, climbing along the rocks on the coast, exploring little inlets, listening to the waves crash up against the rocks. I enjoyed myself immensely for quite a while until it was time to start heading back. I hadn't brought any sustenance with me, so I knew I was about to get hungry. But I didn't want to head back the same way I came. I'm much more of a loop adventurer than an out-and-back adventurer. There are more fun and exciting things to see that way.

I found a path that went along the rocks by the water, assuming that it would go all around and lead me back to Hondoq Bay. (I was, after all, on an island). If I could get there, I would know my way back up to the villa.

My assumption, however, was very incorrect.

The path I was walking suddenly ended at this massive rock quarry where they were tearing up the earth and turning it into stones and gravel. Probably not the safest place to be on foot with sandals on. I got a little worried and feared someone seeing me where I wasn't supposed to be. I snuck up the hill to the right, assuming and hoping it would lead me to another main road up and around it. I didn't quite know where I was, but I knew I just needed to go up.

Again, my assumption was incorrect. Another dead end. I was usually much better at navigating than this.

As I was standing up there, wondering what to do next (still stubbornly refusing to just go back the way I came), I saw a huge front loader tractor come slowing rolling up the hill towards me. Perfect. I tried to start walking down in hopes I could somehow avoid this inevitable interaction and get in trouble. I tried to run away. Well, that didn't work, and the interaction came but in a way that I wasn't expecting.

The man driving the tractor stopped the roaring engine when he pulled up right next to me and started talking to me in Maltese of which I understood nothing.

'Umm, do you speak English?' I asked.

He stared at me.

'I am lost.'

He nodded.

I had to figure out how to ask him if he could point me in the right direction. I am pretty terrible at learning other languages. I think I'm just incapable of doing it. I want it to be perfect right away, so I won't even try if I know I'm going to butcher the pronunciation. You'd think for someone who had travelled so much, I'd gotten used to it. But I didn't. I still suck at it.

I remembered that I had an email I could pull up on my phone which had the address of the villa. I showed him the address. I couldn't remember how to pronounce the name of the town and I wanted to make sure there was no misunderstanding as to where I wanted to go. I needed to get to Qala. (Take your best guess at pronouncing it … it might be wrong. Maybe not. Who knows?)

With an understanding nod after looking at the address, he invited me to climb up the steps of the tractor and hold on tight. He said, in broken English, that he could drive me over to the other side of the quarry and there would be a road that would lead me to another road that would lead me in the right direction. Standing on the small platform just outside the door, I felt the cool breeze of an air-conditioned cabin, and I was happy.

'Thank you so much for the ride. I really appreciate it. My name is Kellie.'

'You're welcome. I'm Simon.'

'Nice to meet you, Simon.'

What a nice guy.

I'm sure he was quite curious about what the heck a twenty-five-year-old blonde girl from a land-locked state in America was doing in his rock quarry on a tiny island in the middle of the Mediterranean Sea. I attempted to explain the ship in its simplest terms which was always a challenging endeavour to embark upon even if we speak the same language. I'm not sure he understood a word.

We reached the other side of the quarry after a few bumpy minutes, and he showed me the road he had mentioned. I thanked him again for the ride and the momentary cool air, descended the steps to the ground, and we parted ways.

My initial hope at finding my way home was dashed quite quickly when this road came to yet another dead end with no alternative pathways in sight. None at all. Just bushes. And my new friend Simon was heading back to work. Resolved to push on, my excellent sense of direction finally kicked in and I knew which way I had to go: up and to the left. Into the bushes, thorns, and weeds I went, scraping up my legs along the way. This continued for a solid forty-five minutes, all the while constantly asking myself, 'Where is the flipping road?'

Finally, some semblance of a path emerged beneath my feet, so I just stayed on it through the overgrown bushes. To my great relief, a road! An actual road. I took a guess at which direction to go and for the first time all day, my instinct was correct. I started to recognise my surroundings again and knew I would be home soon, and I could finally have some lunch.

Later that afternoon, we piled in the truck and took a short drive to Hondoq Bay. I was annoyed that I hadn't been able to find my way there along the coast. We went swimming anyways.

All around a good adventure day.

On Seasickness

DATE: August 2014
LOCATION: Malta
      35° 59' 36.3" N
      14° 26' 35.7" E

When you're seasick, everything in life sucks.

Like, really sucks.

Just picture yourself sitting outside on the deck of a boat in gloomy weather that is rocking you up and down, forward and back, side to side, with your stomach going in those same directions deep inside of you but just a second behind, always trying to catch up or resist. That delicious dinner you just ate doesn't want to stay down. Your insides are churning angrily, your eyes tired, your head pounding and disoriented, your abs fully engaged attempting to keep you upright, your ears throbbing from all the noise of the wind and waves, and your nose curling at the smells of exhaust coming out right next to you as you hover over the rail. Every little movement seems to make it all so much worse. Getting out of bed to put your shoes and jacket on is no longer a simple task; it now requires every mental, emotional and physical ability you possess to accomplish.

And the worst part is – you have no idea when it will end.

All you can think about when you're seasick is how much you don't want to feel sick anymore. All you can focus on is the pain you feel and the deepest desire of your heart to make it stop. You don't want to answer to anyone, you don't want to do, say or eat anything. You don't want to move. All you want, and sometimes literally all you can do, is to just lie there, close your eyes and hope it all ends soon.

At times, it feels like if it would just come up already, you could get it over with and be better. Sometimes that does make things better, but standing on the rail with half your body hanging over it to the leeward side to avoid all that comes spewing from your mouth to go anywhere on yourself – or in the unfortunate open porthole beneath your line of fire – isn't a fun experience either. Especially if nothing actually comes out no matter how hard you try. Trust me, when there's nothing left in your stomach to throw up but bile, it's way worse than if there was something more. I'd even take those dreaded tomatoes over nothing. (I'd still draw the line at vegetable crisps and capers though …).

There is little anyone around you can do to help. Sure, they can give you a cup of water, a towel to clean any leftovers off your face, or a piece of toast to refill your stomach. They could try to distract and encourage you that the two of you were just really bonding in that moment by going through this awful experience together. It might make you smile, maybe even laugh, but it doesn't take the pain away.

Again, when you're seasick, everything in life sucks.

Really sucks.

But there is something to always be redeemed with seasickness.

As odd as that might sound.

Eventually, it stops. Eventually, you find your balance. Eventually, the ship will slow down, the rocking will cease and the feeling will pass. And when that moment comes, life suddenly becomes beautiful again. Glorious even. It truly is the best feeling in the world to have gotten though the seasickness to the point when you simply don't feel sick anymore. Your stomach settles, you can breathe, you can move, you can laugh, and you can't help but smile. The simple tasks that took every effort you possessed to accomplish suddenly seem so easy and you enjoy them so much more than you ever had. You recognize the things you've always taken for granted.

And it's because of one simple realisation – you just don't feel sick anymore.

I had just been spending a month enjoying the relaxed Mediterranean island life on Gozo and it was time to re-join crew on Next Wave. The ship was sailing into Malta for a pit stop before going to Gozo so the family I had been staying with and I went over to Malta to greet them. We sat on the quayside of where they would be coming alongside and I eagerly watched for her sails to come around the corner. I watched Next Wave getting closer and closer and was there to grab the mooring lines when they threw them down to lock in place. After a few months on land, I was about to be a sailor again.

I hopped on board and was welcomed with open arms back to my home. After restocking some supplies, we set course for Gozo, which was a pretty short distance away. On our port side, we'd pass by St. Paul's Bay which is where Paul had shipwrecked in the book of Acts, so that was pretty cool.

On this short sail, winds were pretty strong and the swell quite large. That's an ideal combination for a rocky ride. Having spent the previous couple months living on land, I wasn't feeling so great with all the extra movement.

I sat on the port side deck with my back against the wheelhouse feeling like death. Dramatic, maybe, but it's honestly a pretty good description. Not only was I physically sick, but I also started to relate it to my own mental and emotional state. This whole seasick thing was not just a sailing thing but a life thing.

I had felt seasick often. (And I'm not talking anymore about being on a boat in stormy seas). There were so many days, weeks, and months when all I could focus on was how sick I felt: stress, anger, unhappiness, confusion, hurt. I ached every day. The things I once enjoyed didn't seem so great anymore, and I couldn't appreciate them like I used to. I was burnt out. I didn't always want to be where I was, I didn't always want to be doing what I was doing. I often just wanted to go home. I wanted everything to just be good, but I couldn't will it to be.

I think we all go through seasons like this in life. Seasons of just feeling off. Seasons of feeling pretty hopeless. And in those seasons, it's so easy to perpetually focus on the negative, focus on what's not going the way you want, what's not going right. I go through those seasons seemingly more often than not. I can get pretty low real quick. And what's even more frustrating is it tends to come when, on the outside, life should seem pretty good. Flipping heck, I was living on a boat, travelling to some incredible places, experiencing things I never even dreamed of, but I had such a hard time getting out of my head to enjoy it – I couldn't always see the good. That frustrated the crap out of me.

Because all I could focus on was how awful I felt.

Feeling like death on this sail, I remembered something, though. I remembered there would be that moment when I wasn't sick anymore. I remembered that it was always a glorious occasion. It was coming.

So, sitting against the side of the wheelhouse with my head down on my knees, tears streaming down my face, trying to keep as still as I could on the rocking boat, trying to stop my spinning thoughts and stomach, I remembered the part about seasickness being temporary. I remembered that there was going to be that moment when I suddenly wasn't sick anymore, when I wouldn't be angry, frustrated, stressed or unhappy, and the world would be bright again, when the confusion would become clear and the hurt, healed.

Remembering the hope for that glorious moment, I looked up from my huddled position on deck to see the horizon in front of me. It was gone. I didn't feel nauseous anymore. Tears dried up as I realised I could get up and move. I could breathe. I could walk.

In that moment of looking up, I knew there was hope. Hope for redemption. I wasn't going to be seasick in life forever. It would pass, and when it did, I knew that I would be able to appreciate this life that God so graciously gave me to live so much more than had I not experienced the hell of seasickness. I would be able to enjoy the crap out of where I was, who I was with, and what I was doing. I would be able to make the most of it. I knew there was going to be another sail on the horizon, another storm to pass, another bout of seasickness to overcome, but I also knew that redemption was possible. I was catching glimpses of it more and more every day.

Dry Dock

DATE: August 2014
LOCATION: Paola, Malta
 35° 52' 48.4" N
 14° 30' 55.6" E

One time were locked in an oven for three weeks.

Malta is a hot and humid place during the summer, as previously mentioned too many times. This could often be tolerated by taking a dip into the sea (which I did every day) or standing directly below the air conditioner right outside my cabin door. But outside, there was no escape. What made it exponentially hotter was being in dry dock – what felt like a literal oven.

We were scheduled to do some important repairs and maintenance to the hull of Next Wave which could only be done by taking the ship completely out of the water. This was quite a process to witness. We slowly manoeuvred into dock number five near Paola, just south across Grand Harbour in Valetta, and they closed the metal doors behind us. Then, the sea started to recede beneath us. With the water level dropping, we slowly came to rest on a line of blocks to be perfectly balanced upright and keep ourselves in place. Resting in just the right spot, the steady movement of the ship ceased and she was still. A little while later, the water was completely gone, and we would be able to walk on dry ground and see the ship from a very different perspective. The only thing was that we were incredibly high off the ground. Our gangway seemed tiny compared to our height off the ground out of water now.

A three-story staircase was assembled on our port side. Yes, three stories. This was both a blessing and a curse. A blessing because it was an easy way to get on and off. A curse because the only way for us to have fresh water on board was to purchase six-pack cases of two-litre water bottles. We stocked up with as much as we possibly could, filling the forward hull in the skansen to the brim. We had about twenty-four people on board, so we went through a lot of water. But carrying those cases up all those stairs in the heat of summer surrounded by metal walls that radiated the heat even more (like an oven) was no easy feat. We tried an assembly line up the stairs if enough people were available. We even tried throwing a rope down, tying the case to it, and hoisting it up. Either method we tried required a lot of heavy lifting.

We got right to work as soon as the water dried up beneath us. The following three weeks consisted of repairing the bow thruster, removing rust, and repainting the hull (including the rudder), cleaning the propeller, unravelling and detangling the entire length of both anchor chains, re-sewing some sails and a few other projects. We did everything we could to take advantage of the boat being out of the water and work on things in areas we couldn't usually reach.

———— ⦔ ————

When I had taken my break in England, I found out that my friend, Sidney, was getting married and she wanted me to stand beside her on the big day they had set for January. I knew I had to do everything I could to make it there, despite my serious lack of funds. Not only might I be able to be at my friend's wedding, but I realised I could also be home for Christmas, something I had missed the previous three years – and I didn't want there to be a fourth. I mean, the last three Christmases had been amazing, each memorable in their own way including a midnight service at the Liverpool Cathedral, lots of Christmas carols, homemade stockings and swimming. But there's nothing like being home for Christmas.

The reality of my serious lack of funds hit me when I was given a bill for crew fees. It had added up to over 1,000 euros that I owed, or about $1,500. On top of that, a round trip flight across the pond was going to cost another $1,000, plus travel to and from Kentucky for the wedding would add a few hundred dollars more. I had no idea how I was going to come up with that amount of money. I was an estimated $2,000 short for this endeavour.

After feeling incredibly discouraged, I decided to do all I could to try to raise the money. I planned to create a fundraiser online as well as make a short video asking for help. Visuals were always nice and helpful for others to catch a small glimpse of what my life looked like. In between the hours spent outside working on the hull and untwisting the anchor chain, I managed to record and put together a video and prepare this fundraiser to be posted.

I took a $2, twenty-minute bus ride to the airport with my computer to post it. There were hardly any places nearby with decent internet access, so the airport was the best place for this. I shared the fundraiser with everyone I could, but my video wouldn't upload so that would have to wait. Despite the airport being the best internet, it still wasn't great.

Within ten minutes of sharing the fundraiser, someone had given $15. Hope sparked. I had sat there for about an hour trying to get the video to upload before I had to give up and head back. But by that time, I already had $115 donated. Hope and excitement ignited at the thought that this could all actually happen. That I would really be able to go home to Colorado for Christmas and to Kentucky for a wedding. Money kept steadily coming in that day, and I was so incredibly grateful every time I checked my email to see someone else had donated more, no matter the amount.

Later that night, I went out with a few other crew members to a small café with a very large and loud bingo game going on outside. And by large, I mean table after table of Maltese men and women of all ages playing bingo on the dirt lawn. Amidst the numbers being called out and screams that someone got a bingo, the video finally uploaded, and all there was left to do was wait and hope.

Our time in dry dock was coming to an end, and we would soon be back in the water and heading to Gozo. Before that happened though, we had a birthday to celebrate which included a dance party in the dock and the *best* chocolate cake I have ever tasted. We called it Glory to Glory Cake. It was so glorious to eat that you could just die, and then you'd be in glory in heaven afterward. All good things, really.

Two weeks later, I sat at a small corner table at Horatio's Tavern in Gozo, overlooking Mgarr Marina, having a glass of wine, with my debit card in hand about to purchase a flight home. In those two weeks, I had been given enough money to book the four flights I needed and to get caught up on all my crew fees. Again, it only took *two weeks* for all of this to happen. I was so amazed and so thankful for God's provision through family and friends.

In the midst of my seasickness, when I was huddled on the deck feeling miserable, God was up to something good. And not just in me but on the other side of the world with every person that felt led to give.

God is good to his kids. He knows our needs, wants, and desires, and he wants to fulfil all of those in incredible ways that we can't begin to understand. We more often than not just have to wait for his timing.

In Pieces

DATE: September 2014
LOCATION: Gozo
      36° 1' 38.5" N
      14° 18' 16.4" E

The first week of any DTS is always full and busy. This week was no exception. It was the very first week of the Bluewater DTS. It was a time to introduce the newcomers to what they were about to jump into aboard Next Wave.

About six months before this first week, I felt God put a challenge on my heart to prepare a teaching on hearing God's voice. This was for sure a challenge because that was something I felt ill-equipped to even talk about let alone teach. It had been a struggle for me since my own DTS nearly four years prior. It was something I had been continuing to learn along the way. I didn't always understand it. I felt like an imposter attempting to teach it to someone. I was intimidated just by the idea of putting together some semblance of a teaching. So, I didn't do it.

I would have many moments of feeling like that in the months to come – moments of feeling ill-equipped. I was taking on a challenge as I had never experienced before. Most of the time, I had no idea what I was doing. I just did it.

The first week included a lot of different kinds of teachings to introduce the basics of what would be covered in the months to come. I was putting together the schedule of who would be teaching what topics throughout the week. Daniel and Tamara were visiting for the week to help get things started, so I asked Daniel if he could teach this topic of hearing God's voice. It was something I felt to be a really important concept, and I knew he could do it justice far better than I could. But that night, as I lay in bed getting ready to go to sleep, that challenge came back around. I knew in my gut that God wanted me to do it instead. I couldn't deny it anymore, and I couldn't get out of it this time. I had to do it.

The next morning, I walked over to Daniel and said, 'Never mind, Daniel, looks like I'll be doing the hearing God's voice teaching.'

He looked at me, said nothing and just smiled. It's like he knew.

I had really come to enjoy teaching. I thought I was pretty good at it, especially when it was a topic I felt I had a good grasp on. But at the beginning of putting these thoughts on the page about hearing God's voice, I started to worry. I kept looking through other sources for what I should say. I looked back at my own notes I had taken during other teachings on the subject, some books, and other people's teaching outlines. It was all good stuff and points that I thought were good, important and necessary to include in my own teaching.

But I started doing something that never led anywhere good – I was shoulding all over myself. (Yes, it's supposed to sound like a different word …)

That term was coined by a very wise woman named Anne, and it dug deep into my brain and stayed there. She spoke on identity, and I had heard her teaching enough times to know what was coming next. So often we are creatures of 'should'. We should do this. We should do that. We should be like this. We should think like that. We should all over ourselves and beat ourselves up when things aren't lining up the way they should. But we're not meant to live in the 'should'.

Recognising the should I was falling into, I put away all the notes I had surrounding me across the table. I closed the books containing others' thoughts and ideas. I realised I didn't need any of those. I knew in my heart how I heard God's voice and the truths that resonated with me and what the Bible said on the subject. God put it on my heart to do this for a reason because he wanted to use my words and experience to show others that they could also hear God's voice.

I stopped looking around me and looked in. I added my own flavour to it. And that flavour involved puzzles.

I wanted to talk about puzzles.

I love puzzles.

I really love puzzles.

I'm really good at them.

I had discovered how God spoke to me through puzzles.

―――――⟵⟵―――――

When I first went to England in 2011, there was a small group of us who shared a common interest in puzzles. After nearly every mealtime in BB Hall at YWAM Harpenden, we would work together on a puzzle, quite often late into the night. We bonded over those hours of putting pieces together, bringing out a new one the moment we finished. I started to recognise the different ways people went about putting the pieces together in front of them. Some would grab one and compare it to the bigger picture to figure out exactly where it belonged on the table and place it there. Others, like me, worked more with patterns and colours to put a section together and then find its home.

I am not a big picture person, I'm much more in the details. Big picture, intuitive thinking, stresses me out. So, looking at the hundreds of tiny pieces scattered across the table could easily overwhelm me. But when I looked at just the details, when I looked for just a specific colour or pattern, I'd start to see the pieces I needed, collect them and put them together. I had all the pieces, I just had to start somewhere. Working on one pattern would bring in another, so then I'd look for those pieces to continue building on what I had already put together. After I was satisfied with my progress, I could take a moment to step back, look at what I had put together, see what it was and put it in its place.

Putting together a puzzle is a process. Sometimes – well, most times – a very long process requiring patience and a desire to work at it and trust that you will see the result eventually.

Pretty much everything in my life is a process much like this. One piece at a time. I don't always know where all the pieces go in the beginning. But there I sit. Night after night. Connecting the pieces. Waiting in anticipation to put the final piece in.

One day, my friend Sidney said something that stuck with me. She said, 'God knows how you do your puzzles.'

He knows because he wired me that way.

Through those puzzles in BB Hall, I realised that was the way God tended to work in my life. I had gathered a wide range of experiences and skills that, on their own, didn't make sense in the grand scheme of things. But when I could take a step back, I could see how the pieces of my life fit together and how one piece prepared me for the next.

Through those puzzles, I realised God would put the pieces together of whatever I was going through. Sometimes, he'd say something directly; others, it came from taking a second to stop my overthinking tendencies and focus on something else for a moment. It was when my mind was clearer and calmer that I could listen and think better. Doing a puzzle was one way to clear my overactive mind. It became a way I could find time and headspace to process things.

Through those puzzles, I realised that we serve an incredibly creative God who wants a relationship with us. So much so that he'll speak to us through our favourite things. He speaks differently to each person. He is so creative that each of us hear and comprehend and act in all different ways which he has created specifically for us.

For some, God speaks clearly and directly. Some in Scripture, some in songs, others in questions. Some in their gut.

God speaks to me in pieces. (And my gut but mostly pieces.)

It was through this process of putting together puzzles that I began to understand and recognise God's voice in my own life. I am incredibly confident in the way I do my puzzles. As I said, I'm pretty freaking good at them.

So, I began to ask the question, What if I could be as confident in the ways God speaks to me as I am in doing puzzles?

With a blank page in front of me, I started penning my thoughts on puzzles. When I stopped *shoulding*, I began to get excited. I realised that I actually did know what I was talking about, and it gave me so much more confidence in my ability to teach on the subject. God clearly had it in mind for me to do that specific teaching for that group. I had learned how to know and recognise his voice and was fully capable of showing others how to do the same.

My artistic creativity comes out maybe once a year, so I'm glad I saved it for this moment. I grabbed an outdated navigational chart of the coast of Sicily from the drawer stocked full of charts mapping areas all over Europe and decided to turn it into a puzzle. To make it even cooler and to get some of my main points across, I water-coloured the whole thing with a wide range of colours, adding salt before it dried for added texture and pattern. It was awesome. Once all the paint had dried, I wiped off the salt and layered on a bunch of Mod Podge. When that dried, I drew out my puzzle lines on the back. My excitement for this teaching grew.

While watching one of my favourite movies on the floor of the saloon next to a bowl of popcorn, I made my cuts with a blunt razor blade, and a legit puzzle emerged. One of a kind. And pretty flipping cool. I mixed up all the pieces so I could practice putting them together. I was giddy.

My plan was to begin the teaching by putting the puzzle together up on the whiteboard with blue tack, explaining the way I did puzzles as I attempted it. It turns out that it's hard to do a puzzle in front of a group of people while simultaneously trying to remember what I was supposed to be talking about. It's also hard when there wasn't quite enough blue tack and the pieces kept falling to the floor. I eventually had to just give up on the puzzle which was incredibly irritating, but I just had to stop looking at it. Pretty sure they got the point I was trying to make.

The whole premise of that teaching was to show that we are all fully capable of hearing the voice of God and that he speaks to each one of us in all different and creative ways. That he wants us to hear his voice. That he just wants a relationship with us.

For God does speak – now one way, now another – though man may not perceive it.
Job 33:14

I got to see all of their faces at the end of my teaching when they realised that they could hear God's voice too, that he cared for them and wanted to speak to them and wanted them to hear him.

This concept of hearing God's voice had been a struggle for me for years. I always felt like I just didn't get it, I didn't understand it, couldn't figure it out. But in that moment, it all came full circle. I had been taught how, piece by piece, moment by moment, and I got to teach others the same thing. There were so many others with more experience and could probably have taught that topic far better than I ever could. But God wanted me to have that moment of seeing how far I had come.

My number of redemption points was steadily increasing.

Sea Shanty Night

DATE: September 2014
LOCATION: Gozo
36° 1' 38.5" N
14° 18' 16.4" E

I've mentioned The Baltic Fleet being one of my favourite pubs, right? It was just a ten-minute walk away from where we had been moored at Albert Dock in Liverpool, England. I came to love it not just for its proximity to where we lived or its delicious pints of cider on tap but for what happened one night a month.

A sea shanty night.

A sea shanty is a song that sailors of old would sing to keep motivated and entertained while working hard on ships. (You've heard a few if you've ever seen the movie, *Master and Commander*.) These were always story songs. Songs that passed the time, held a beat to keep them in sync when pulling lines and raising sails on a tall ship, and reminded them of home. At The Baltic Fleet, this sea shanty night would bring in so many people of all ages, though mostly older, to come with their accordions and concertinas to sing these songs together. When one song ended, someone else would start up another one in a different corner of the crowded room. This went on for hours. And it was wonderful.

It was one of Daniel and Tamara's last night's in Gozo visiting us on the ship before they headed home, and we thought it would be fun to all gather and sing sea shanties and folk songs. We wanted to re-create our own version of The Baltic Fleet's Sea Shanty Night (though unfortunately without the pints – being a dry ship and all ... We could get our pints later at Horatio's Tavern or The Monkey's Fist ...) A plan was made, treats prepared and songs practiced. Zhenya and her accordion, Santiago, along with others of her family kicked it off with a few songs. Interspersed between them, I was setting the mood with Gaelic Storm songs in the background while people grabbed snacks and switched performers.

One shanty that had become a favourite among many was the famous pirate song all about how great it was being a pirate, a pirate, a pirate except when you lost some body parts. It's all fun and games until that happens ... Tamara and I got up to sing this together. The verses speak of losing ears, eyes, hands, legs, and whatsits. (We decided to do the PG version and left out that last verse ... plus, Tamara and I don't have that certain part, so we wouldn't be able to give the verse the justice it required in performance ...).

Daniel stood up next and brilliantly delivered a famous poem. It was met with mixed reactions of both laughter and sadness at its contents. It was a poem about a sad polar bear. This poor polar bear had lost its family on a particular iceberg that was hit by a really big ship in 1912 and this polar bear was desperately searching for them. It's a story that still gets me every time. He never found them.

The night ended with two classic songs. 'The Leaving of Liverpool', and 'Drunken Sailor'. 'The Leaving of Liverpool' bringing back nostalgic memories of our time spent in the great city of Liverpool, as well as the parting of ways of fellow crew members.

It was definitely a night to remember.

Thunderstorms Roll In

DATE: September 2014
LOCATION: Gozo
36° 1' 38.5" N
14° 18' 16.4" E

Running in wellies is a mistake. Especially when those wellies are one size too big. Don't ever do it. Take my word for it.

Sometimes, autumn in the Med can bring with it some interesting weather. We were just sitting in our nice, quiet marina in Gozo on a beautiful Mediterranean afternoon. The sun set as it usually does with its beautiful colours fading beneath the hills. Just after dinner, I looked off into the distance to see flashes of lightning, signs of a storm heading our way.

About an hour later, *Pirates of the Caribbean* was playing on the TV (because living on a boat means you should probably watch any and all movies relating to ships, sailing, and/or pirates). I wasn't really in the mood to watch a movie though, plus I kept catching glimpses of the sky being lit up by the lightning through the small windows lining the saloon. I decided to go upstairs to sit out on deck and watch. It was a beautiful sight to see, though there were several times my head hurt from the intense brightness of the constant flashes. After about an hour or so out on deck, watching the storm build around me, the rains finally caught up to us. There were suddenly huge raindrops barrelling down on me. Time to go inside.

Minutes after being in the safety of the wheelhouse, the rains came with a vengeance. As did the wind. But mostly the rain. It was raining so heavily that there was a cloud of mist along the surface of the water surrounding us. This was a horrible time to have had those two cups of cranberry juice sloshing around in my system. I had to pee, which was incredibly irritating and terribly inconvenient.

Why was I so irritated at this very natural and important bodily function? Well, remember a while ago when we were given back the luxury of being able to flush the toilet every time? Like most things on a ship, it takes a lot of work to keep all things running as they should. And things on a boat just tend to break. This was unfortunately one of those times, and our toilets had been completely out of commission for an entire month. This meant we had to take a five-minute walk across the marina to the toilets on shore any time we needed to relieve ourselves. For that month, I really had to be conscious of the timing of my liquid consumption.

I was irritated because I knew I was about to get wet. Really wet.

When I announced this great need to the others in the wheelhouse (because this kind of discussion was normal for us ...), Tamara reminded me of the wet weather sailing gear I had in my possession – she gave me trousers months before that I had yet to use. Brilliant. I dug out my trousers, jacket and wellies and braced myself for a trek in the rain.

Several others decided to come with me (the power of suggestion), so it turned into an adventure to the toilets. I was soaked within seconds of being outside in this torrential downpour. Walking briskly down the gangway, along the length of the pontoon, through the gate, up the stairs and down the path to the toilets, I found some really great pools of water begging to be disturbed by a great leap. I jumped from one puddle to the next all the way to the shore toilets. Upon reaching our destination, I came to discover two things: (a) those trousers were awesome, and I was completely dry underneath, and (b) there were no lights on in the building. It happened occasionally that there would be no power in those bathrooms, so I wasn't too surprised. Especially when considering the conditions. Just another inconvenience to add to the list. It was becoming comical by this point. It was time to take a pee in the dark. I left the stall door more than slightly ajar to catch the consistent flashes of lightning which would light up the stall just enough to be able to find my seat and then see where the toilet paper was. There were a couple of us in this same predicament, so laughter abounded among us.

After everyone was relieved, we braced ourselves to head back into the storm. By this point, my jacket was no longer blocking any water from seeping through. It was too wet for it to handle any more. It was fun at first, but I was over it and ready to be out of the rain. I started running. After about thirty seconds of running, my foot came down at the wrong angle and writhed with pain. I had a hard time putting any pressure at all on it. I limped the rest of the way back to the end of the dock towards the boat in the heavy rain. I wasn't having fun anymore.

Like I said, running in wellies is stupid.

I immediately put on some dry clothes when I was back in the safety of our four walls. My lower half was incredibly dry but the same could not be said for my upper half. Warmed up and dried out, I went back up to the wheelhouse to keep watching the storm surrounding us. It was almost as if we were all on watch again. I was surrounded by familiar faces of crew members I had known for years and faces I had just met that week.

With the sounds of the wind and rain, the movement of the boat, the talk of sailing, and the darkness of night, it was a reminder of past sails, past experiences, and it was good. Really good. Daniel moved to a seat behind the helm and took the usual perch there. Tamara was standing next to him in front of the valve that controls the revving of the engine, I was sitting in the chair in the starboard corner, and the others on the seats in front of the stairs next to the radar. All the while, Anthony kept going in and out of the rain, checking on the mooring lines and just running around as happy as could be. It was a good moment. One I can still vividly picture in my mind.

After sitting and enjoying the moment for a bit, the pain in my ankle started to become much more apparent. I went down to get an ice pack and came back to my seat. It didn't last long until the pain was too much, and I decided it was time for me to go to sleep. That was a good call, as much as I wanted to stay in that moment watching the storm with some of my favourite people. I took some ibuprofen, ankle propped on an ice pack and pillow, and I went to sleep.

A week or so later, it had been a pleasant Sunday with very little happening. People were relaxing in all parts of the saloon, enjoying having the day with no responsibilities. It was finally lunchtime, so I entered the galley to fry up some leftover rice with some eggs. I noticed through the little galley porthole that it had become dark and grey outside quite suddenly. Not thinking too much of it, I sat down at the first corner table overlooking the saloon to enjoy my meal. It was my favourite spot in the room. A few bites into lunch, a major gust blew outside, and the boat started heeling over to port.

Kyrah and I looked at each other for just a second across the table, communicating everything we needed to in that glance, then jetted outside to see what was going on. Another storm was suddenly on top of us with heavy winds from the south and rain racing down from above and lightning flashes going off in all directions. It came out of nowhere. Everyone (well, everyone who was awake) immediately jumped into action, going to all parts of the deck checking that everything was secure, getting clothes off the drying lines outside, tightening the safety of our mooring lines, hoping to secure our small sailing dinghy next to us in the water so that its mast didn't ram into our hull, and Anthony up on the gaff tying the mainsail down even more.

At one point, I noticed Kyrah needing help getting the fire hose down that had been hanging out to drain on a halyard, so I ran over to help. After untying it from the railing, I let go of my end and the line and hose started to fall fast towards the water. Both Kyrah and I exclaimed the same expletive at the same time, thinking we'd lose it to the sea below in the chaos. Luckily, she had hold of the other side of the hose, and I had grabbed back the other line, so we didn't lose it – all the while, the rain was pounding hard on our faces. When we got the hose completely down, we just looked at each other and started laughing at the ridiculousness of the situation, then we looked around us to see what else needed to be done.

With the mooring lines secure, we all went back inside to get out of the wet and watch the storm from the comfort of the wheelhouse. It was not quite as relaxing and enjoyable as the last thunderstorm though. Just in front of us was the entrance to the marina where a whole lot of boats (ferries, sailing boats, motorboats, and fancy yachts) were frantically racing to find safety in the harbour. The Blue Lagoon was a popular tourist destination on the island of Camino just off the coast of Gozo but had no shelter from weather like this. We watched as small motorboats went airborne through the massive waves, desperately trying to get to the marina without being capsized. The craziest though was the ferry boats crashing down with the biggest splashes on either side coming in our direction. It was almost like watching those crazy videos of cargo ships in a storm in the middle of the ocean.

One of those fancy yachts came to make berth next to us on the other side of our pontoon. They hadn't called the harbour office, so they didn't have a spot set aside for them. They were just trying to find a place to rest and be safe from the storm anywhere they thought they could. It was a family of three who had been out enjoying their day before the sky turned grey. As they were attempting to tie up next to the pontoon, several of our crew offered to jump down to help grab their lines for them. For some stupid reason, they refused our help. They probably didn't want us young folks messing with their fancy paint job.

That was their first mistake.

There was another yacht on the pontoon in front of them, so there wasn't quite enough space for them to tie up properly. As they tried to come in, the wind picked up again and started pushing them back. They kept getting pushed backward which resulted in them inching closer towards our ship and even closer to our small sailing dinghy. They tried to kick their stern out so they could turn away but as they did that, their bow veered towards us and our dinghy, as well as our mooring lines. It wasn't looking good.

The bow of their yacht started scraping against the side of our little dinghy, which then snapped the small mast in three places from the pressure. Things kept escalating. They then started dragging on our mooring line. This would have been bad seeing how it was the most important line that was stopping us from swinging to hit the other very nice and expensive yachts on our port side. That would not have been good had that line been damaged. He somehow got off of our lines and further away from us, which was good, though our dinghy had irreparable damage to it. I was surprised it was still afloat by the looks of it. They tried again to come alongside the pontoon. This time, finally realising they needed our help to come alongside.

They managed to finally get the fancy yacht tied up securely through the battering of the wind and rain. The fancy yacht guy came over and said to us, 'Whatever it costs to fix that sail dinghy, I'll cover it.' Apparently, he was some sort of famous Maltese actor whom none of us had ever heard of.

I finally returned to my cold bowl of fried rice to finish eating, watch a movie and take the occasional walk outside to double-check the mooring lines were still secure through the duration of the rough weather.

It is because of moments like these that I still feel the need to jump up and secure things outside whenever a storm comes in, no matter where I am. I always have to then stop myself and calm down, remembering that nothing was going to blow away. But I'm always ready in case things really do blow away.

Shley on the Mainsail

DATE: October 2014
LOCATION: Gozo to Sicily
      36° 38' 58.9" N
      13° 38' 20.1" E

I had become accustomed to nothing going according to plan. So, when something happened on the day it was originally scheduled to happen, it felt like a freaking miracle. A miracle happened when we left Gozo to sail for Sicily. We left on the exact day we had planned months before, and I was shocked. And very happy about it. We were sailing with our new crew and new trainees, and it was a beautiful day.

One aspect of living on a boat is that it often requires people to stare their fears in the face. But it also allows for a plethora of opportunities to overcome them. Sometimes that fear comes when you're finally leaving for a new destination and you have to drive the motor dinghy out into open waters to meet up with the ship and the waves are big and you almost flip over from the height you reach because you're going quite fast and the wind catches your bow. Sometimes it's different ...

An important task during any sail is to untie the mainsail. Along the length of the sail were small ropes called sail ties which wrapped around the gaff and the rolled up sail to help keep it in place. Once untied, it freed it to be able to raise when we needed it. But to complete that task, you had to harness up and manoeuvre up on top of the gaff. With each sail tie loosed, you would inch your way forward to the next one and so on until all the sail ties were loose.

Our mainsail was about ten or so feet above the deck. And on a moving ship, that can be high enough to freak out anyone trying to accomplish this task while keeping their balance. But for those with a fear of heights, it's enough for them to freeze in place.

Ashley (who I always called Shley) was afraid of heights. Surprisingly, when volunteers were called for to hop up onto the gaff to untie the sail ties, she was among the first few to raise their hands. I was surprised because I knew the courage it took to put her hand up for that. I climbed up on top of the wheelhouse with her to make sure her harness was on correct, that she attached herself to the right safety line along the gaff, and knew how the sail ties worked to untie them. I also went up there to make sure she would be OK – to be there for her if she needed.

She carefully hoisted herself onto the gaff and took a minute to find her bearings and balance. And courage. We were moving with the swell of the sea so this wasn't the easiest task.

'You good, Shley?'

'I think so. Yep.'

'You got this. I'm here if you need.'

'Umm, OK, Coach.'

She untied one and started slowly shuffling her way towards the next.

Then, she kept going until she made it halfway out there to meet in the middle with Anthony who was coming from the other end of the gaff.

She faced her fear.

I'm not sure if she ever wanted to do it again, but the fact alone that she stood up to take that on spoke volumes of who she was.

I had learned the importance of facing your fears not long before this. When I was at my lowest, consumed with anxiety about sailing, I knew I couldn't cower in fear in the Nav office every time the winds picked up. I would have to take that step back out on deck and face it head-on. Which I did.

I understood, at least a little bit, of the fear that was probably raging through Shley's body and mind when she climbed up on that gaff. I watched as she timidly scooted her bum along the beam, doing what she was tasked to do. And I watched as she made it to the middle to meet Anthony with big smiles on both their faces.

I got to watch her face her fears and overcome them. That's a pretty special thing to witness.

Knowing Your Home

DATE: November 2014
LOCATION: Palermo, Sicily
        38° 7' 45.4" N
        13° 22' 9.4" E

There was a day when I realised how much I knew Next Wave, like, really knew it. I knew the ins and outs of that boat like the back of my hand. I could picture every step and bump and post in every part of every deck. I knew when to step up and when to lower my head, and I did it without thinking. I knew how each drawer in the galley opened, by holding the handle and twisting the latch to pull. I knew what was stored beneath every bench (games, hospitality supplies, dishes, life jackets …) and in every cabinet. My hospitality cupboard full of sheets and towels was always incredibly organized and pretty when I was around. I knew what each rope attached to all parts of our rigging was used for. I knew which valves to open on the emergency water pump so we could attach a fire hose outside to be able to spray the deck with sea water for a good deck scrub. I knew where all supplies for any project lived (outdated navigational charts in a bottom drawer I could use to make countless nautical bookmarks). I knew the layout of the skansen with its tiny bathroom, a hold below to hold all the water bottles we could squeeze in there and the shelves of books around the room designed to keep the books in place during a rocky sail.

    I could navigate around all Next Wave with my eyes closed (as unsafe as that might be to actually do in real life …).

    I knew Next Wave.

This realisation hit hard when we had a visitor come on board one day. We hosted visitors often so this was nothing new, but this one particular moment stood out to me. I was chopping some vegetables on the counter in the galley, and this lady came in to wash her coffee mug. With the entrance to the galley being a fire door, there was a one-and-a-half-inch metal bar on the floor. In case of a fire, the door would shut automatically to not let any air in or out. All our fire doors had something like this. Living there, you would come to know this, and it would become an unconscious action to always step up when going through any of these doorways scattered throughout the ship.

Our visitor was understandably unaware of this. She tripped coming in and going out of the galley every time through the duration of her visit. She said that she just couldn't remember it was there.

I couldn't remember the last time I tripped going in or out of the galley or through any of the doorways. I didn't trip because I knew that bar was there. I knew I had to step up. I knew without knowing that I knew.

I am notoriously hard on myself when I don't know things. I always just want to skip to the part where I know what I'm doing – when I've got it all worked out, when I know my place, I know my responsibilities, I know how to do my job. I have always hated the process of getting there because it makes me feel inadequate. But in time, that process would prove to be worth it, and I would finally come to know my stuff. And often without my being aware of it, until a moment like this when some poor visitor would trip and hurt her foot every time she walked into that galley, and I had to remind her to take a step up whenever she went through the doorway.

I began to realise more and more that I finally kind of knew what I was doing. I knew my place, my role, my home. I wouldn't have gotten there had I quit when I wanted to. Through every up and down, every moment of joy and moment of sorrow, that boat had become my home. I loved that it was my home. And I loved that I knew it as home.

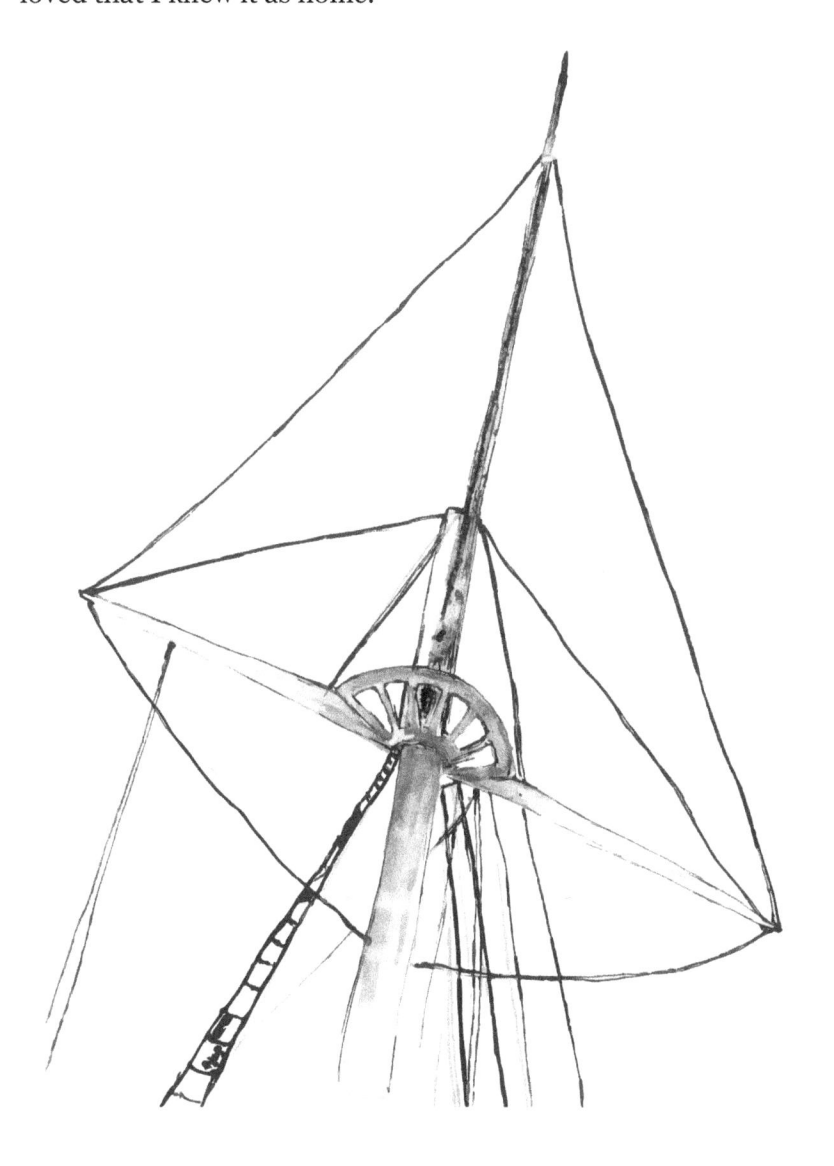

Unfortunate Arrival

DATE: November 2014
LOCATION: Cefalù, Sicily
38° 2' 18.7" N
14° 2' 4.1" E

There are some days in life you look back on and see them as one of your favourite days but for the weirdest of reasons, often because of how terrible and unbelievable the events of the day were. You know those days? Just me? Well, the following twenty-four hours fall into that category.

It was 06:45 one early morning in Sicily as I stepped out onto the quayside to embark on a very long journey. I was setting out to pick up one of our speakers from the airport to bring her back to the ship. Jo was flying into Catania. I was in Palermo, 130 miles away on the other side of the country. The ship was sailing from Palermo to Cefalù that day, 40 miles east of Palermo. My job was to go from Palermo to Catania, back to Palermo, and then on to Cefalù. It was going to be a long day, all 300 miles round trip of it.

The day before this day, we were supposed to have already made our sail to Cefalù. However, due to issues with our water, bunkering for fuel, and the main engine batteries (all very important and necessary functions), sailing had been delayed. Surprise, surprise. So, the plan was for me to pick up Jo at the airport and meet back up with the ship after it had sailed into Cefalù. The timing of it seemed like it would work out well, so we moved forward with that plan.

I had looked at a map to at least have some idea of where I could find the bus station and learned it was going to be a forty-five-minute walk there that morning. (Funny looking back on things like this remembering that a forty-five-minute walk didn't seem too bad.) I left earlier than was needed to give me some extra time. I also had to figure out where we could catch a train to Cefalù when we returned from the airport so I could be prepared. I had learned how to excel at navigating public transportation in foreign countries, which I was incredibly grateful for at that moment, so I wasn't too concerned.

I figured out the right train platform for our ride to Cefalù, so I put that information in my back pocket for later. My next mission was to find the right bus to Catania. If I missed that, I didn't even want to think about what the consequences would have been. There was a sea of buses surrounding me, and I decided it would be better to actually ask someone. The first person I walked up to spoke zero English. I hoped the very little high school Spanish that remained in my brain could prove useful to communicate my need to find a bus to the airport. Autobus, aeropuerto, and Catania were the only words I needed. He pointed me in the right direction. Phew. Special thanks to my favourite high school Spanish teacher for that. (I used more words than those three so don't worry, I've still retained more than just vocab words ...).

I found a small kiosk with the bus company's name, SAIS. I was getting closer. Inside, I thankfully found an English-speaking man behind the glass. However, he went on to tell me that the bus no longer stopped there, so I would have to go around the corner and down another few blocks to get to it. I was slightly confused as I couldn't quite understand much of what he said, though we were speaking the same language. So, I started walking, hoping hard that I would find it in time because if I didn't ... well, I wasn't thinking about that.

To my surprise and delight, around the corner and down a few blocks, I found it. I was anxiously walking down the street and happened to look to my right at the perfect time to see what I needed to see.

With a huge sigh of relief, I stood in line waiting to board. The day was starting off well. I sat on the bus for two and a half hours as it travelled across the heart of Sicily, by the sea and through the mountains. It was quite a beautiful drive. I loved buses. And I loved sitting on buses for long stretches just listening to music, enjoying the view, letting my thoughts wander, and having no other responsibilities in that moment other than to just sit there.

Arriving at the airport, Jo's flight was slightly delayed, so I wandered around the arrivals area for over an hour. I made use of that delay to search for where we would be catching the bus back to Palermo. (Always planning ahead.) When she finally arrived, we went outside to find the bus coming in the next five minutes and made our way to Palermo. This day was going perfectly according to plan, which was always an unlikely event when you lived on a boat, so I enjoyed every moment of it, not even considering that it might have all been too good to be true.

Two and a half hours later, back through the same mountains and next to the same sea, the bus arrived back in Palermo. The next leg of our journey was a train to Cefalù. In that time of sitting on buses and waiting at the airport, Next Wave had set sail from Palermo to Cefalù, so we were heading to meet up with it there. We had no problems getting on the train and enjoyed the view for an hour along the coast towards our destination. By this point, I was hungry. I had only had water all day long, so tiredness was kicking in. But I was still feeling good about how the day had been going.

We got off the train to see a gorgeous city with roads of stone and shops lining the sides of the streets with a towering mountain rising above it all. I finally got service on my phone and tried to get a hold of someone, anyone, on the ship to find out where they were. After a few unanswered calls, they rang me back to let me know they were still an hour or so out from arriving. I wasn't too upset about that because it meant we had time to stop and get some food.

We sat on a bench in the middle of the square enjoying our sandwiches. We had some time to kill, so we took it slow. We decided to start heading our way towards the marina the ship would be pulling into. It was nearing sunset, so we didn't want to have to navigate in the dark.

We stopped at a hill overlooking the marina. We couldn't see her yet, so we took a seat on a ledge overlooking the sea, watching out for my home in the distance. The longer we sat there, the harder it was to see anything. Something was moving in. The dark fog was getting closer and thicker, the winds starting to pick up. By the time darkness nearly set in, I could finally see Next Wave's mast light and green starboard navigational light off in the distance. I knew they were close. And I wished they would hurry.

Finally catching sight of them, Jo and I grabbed our bags and headed down the hill into the marina. We walked down the dock to where she would berth. I saw them turn the corner into the marina just as the weather decided to take a turn for the worse.

I wasn't feeling so good anymore.

I helplessly watched as the wind and waves started beating against the hull, pushing this ice breaker of a steel vessel in all directions except the one it wanted to go with the blackness of night suddenly surrounding us. She would try to move forward to come alongside only to be pushed even farther back. There were too many failed attempts for my liking, and I started to get worried and slightly concerned. I had never seen her struggle like that before. With the wind and rain beating on us, Jo just turned around without a word and started walking the other way. She seemed to have the right idea. I followed in silence.

We found a little office booth to sit next to which allowed us to escape the elements a bit. We watched the ship continue to struggle as the darkness enveloped us. Then, we saw the harbour workers come back towards us, and that worried me even more, telling me that there was a very good chance the ship would not be coming alongside. If those guys weren't out there to grab hold of the lines, that ship wouldn't be sticking around. We were invited inside the booth and just watched in silence as the ship fought to stay in place against the wind. I started considering our options in my mind if we wouldn't be able to get on. We were going to have to find a place to stay that night, and I didn't love the thought of that. I had seen a little hotel along the coast on our walk over to the marina, but I didn't want to have to go down that road.

What we didn't know was at that same moment of my considering other options, a few others were having an adventure of their own of lowering the dinghy into the raging water with two courageous people aboard. I got a phone call from the captain saying they were waiting for us, that when we got on board, we would be going out of the marina to stay the night, just floating around. When I asked how he thought we were going to get on board, he said they were sending the dinghy for us.

In quiet disbelief, I just said OK and hung up. Something about it just didn't seem like a good idea. I looked back towards Next Wave and then saw a man in bright yellow, full wet weather gear, life jacket, and headlamp appearing out of the darkness towards us. He knocked on the door, and I opened it to find a soaking wet Jack with a big smile on his face, telling us we were going with him.

More than slightly concerned, Jo and I hesitantly stood up, and we all raced back through the rain to find the dinghy with a very excited Irish man in the driver's seat, Anthony. With an optimistic greeting in a daunting situation, we loaded into the dinghy with him, ready for a very wet ride. How wet, I would come to very quickly find out. We definitely weren't ready for it. I wasn't, at least. Coming around the first turn of the jetty, the realisation of just how wet I would get in addition to having already been drenched came in a flash. I was sitting on top of the very front tip of the dinghy looking back towards the other three passengers on this crazy adventure together. Suddenly, we hit a wave, rode it up, crashed back down to another wave of frigid seawater just behind it which immediately came up over me, soaking every part of my head and backside and just all over. It happened again and again and again. Laughter was the only response I could come up with as I tried to block Jo from getting as soaked as I was getting by every wave we were consistently hit with. Not sure how effective that was though. But I tried.

This bumpy ride brought us around to the pilot ladder hanging down on the port side, the deck lights being the only light to actually see the ladder. As we approached, with the wind and waves still trying to beat us away, lightning flashing every once in a while over our heads, I reached out for the ladder and grabbed hold with all my might to keep us somewhat in place with the dinghy rising and falling at great heights and going side to side with the swell. We had to time it just right with the swell so that as the dinghy rose up with the waves, we could reach it, balance ourselves standing on the rocking boat and step onto the second rung of the ladder before the swell dropped the dinghy back down several feet below when the ladder would suddenly be nearly out of reach. With that happening pretty consistently, it felt like an extreme balancing act. Jo was up first. She took all this like a champ and immediately went inside when she was safe on deck with the help of others at the top of the ladder on deck. Keeping with the timing of the swell, I sent up Jo's suitcase and then went up myself. Turns out, climbing a ladder when you're beyond drenched head to toe is a lot harder than usual. It adds a bit more weight.

I still don't know how they managed to raise the dinghy that rescued us back to its place on the stern, but they somehow did it. I wasn't part of that operation. I was just done being wet.

Coming downstairs to the saloon dripping wet, I was met with welcoming and excited hellos, as if I hadn't seen everyone in weeks though it had just been the day. After warming up with dry clothes, there was a very large bowl of spaghetti waiting to be consumed, and it was so satisfying.

It was about 18:00 when I sat enjoying my dinner. I got the update on how the night was going to go and they wrote up the watch schedule. Since we were going to be out at sea, not just at anchor, we decided to have all the crew split up into watches through the night to keep the ship and all of us inside safe. Two short hours later, I took the 20:00-00:00 watch with four other crew. We had to keep the ship in a small area designated by the captain. As long as we stayed in that area, we could pretty much do whatever we wanted. We passed the night away by making figure eights through the water to watch our patterns emerge on our computer navigation chart and radar which showed our path. We went in circles all night long and took great joy in our artwork we were 'drawing' on the screen.

At 00:00, I was relieved of duty and finally able to sleep after having had quite the adventure of a day. My head hit the pillow, and I was out. Just not for as long as I wanted. At 06:00, I woke up to the main engine revving just beneath me and the sound of the anchor chain flying down to the depths. The early morning watch had started mooring operations as the sun came up and it was safer to come alongside. The wind was no longer pushing us away.

I went up on deck to find us stern to on the jetty I had been standing on in the wind and rain the night before, unsure of where I'd be sleeping that night. We were bobbing up and down like crazy as the swell continued coming into the rather unprotected marina, but we were tied in and anchored and could attempt to catch back up to our somewhat normal schedule.

That was quite possibly the most eventful twenty-four hours of my life.

———⫷⫷———

For some strange reason, that crazy adventure of a day, that ridiculous night became one of my favourite memories. I can still perfectly picture nearly every moment of that night, standing there helpless and beyond drenched. Living it kind of sucked. I mean, it was pretty terrible. It took everything in me to not just start panicking and getting really pissed off. Watching your home be pushed away from you by the elements is not an ideal situation and one you have zero control over. Racing through raging seas in a small dinghy getting soaked is not an ideal situation. But these were the kinds of situations I had become accustomed to finding myself in, whether I liked it or not.

But instead of panicking, instead of just walking away and giving up and getting angry, I trusted the people around me and trusted my own abilities to do what needed to be done. I saw the adventure in it. I saw the hilarity of it. I saw that I was capable of making it through. So much of that perspective was due to having already made it through some storms before.

I'm sure we all would much rather not have to go through hard things, not have to battle whatever comes against us as we walk through life, not be drenched by wave after wave. But what would it look like to be in the thick of that battle knowing that you're going to get through because you've gotten through before? I know, easier said than done. Trust me, I've had to remind myself of that an absurd amount of times and will probably have to keep doing that throughout the rest of my life. But it's these moments, these experiences, these storms, that shape us into who we are and allow us to walk through the next ones. It wasn't just about finally getting my feet back on deck (which was a welcome conclusion), but what I remember more is how I managed to walk through that entire situation with my head up.

And sometimes, you just have to go with it, no matter how outrageous the way forward is.

Losing to the Sea

DATE: November 2014
LOCATION: Sicily
    38° 1' 56.7" N
    13° 52' 58.1" E

The next day, we had a 'normal' lecture day. Though our definition of normal was certainly not the same as anyone else's normal because, throughout the day, the boat was rocking all over the place and there needed to be someone outside at all times watching the mooring lines in case one (or more) snapped. This had happened a few times already. I even had a horrible dream about that happening. We were moored stern to in a very unprotected port, especially when considering the direction of the wind. It was blowing right at us and carried in some serious swell with it. With only our anchor in the bow and four mooring lines in the stern, we were moving like we were out in open waters. So, to have lectures in that kind of environment was a challenge not many people were up for. Jo had to hold herself steady on a pole to not lose balance during her teaching while some of the trainees started getting seasick just sitting inside, struggling to concentrate.

Later in the day, we had the challenge of putting our gangway out over the stern so we could actually get off to restock some supplies (and frankly just get a break from all the movement). The dinghy was usually hung up there but because we had to get the gangway out, we had to put the dinghy somewhere else for the time being. Attaching the gangway back there proved to be difficult as our stern was going up and down a stupid amount, so the height of the gangway was sometimes so low it crashed on the quayside then so high one had to jump about five feet down to get off. Not ideal. But we made do with what we could. We just had to get really good at timing our getting on and getting off.

The crew had to still be on watches throughout the night to keep an eye on the lines. But this was not to be a very nice night. In the early hours of the morning, we had to make a run for it. Again. I was woken up to an engine revving at a higher speed than I'd ever heard it before. It scared the crap out of me. Especially because the engine was directly below my head on the deck beneath my cabin, so it was real loud when it jolted me awake. I didn't want to get up and see what was going on. I didn't know what to do. With the sounds of the engine working hard, an anchor being raised in a hurry with the noisy hydraulics, the wind pushing us from side to side, and the waves crashing against our hull, it was a little hard to get much rest.

After the ins and outs of sleep, I finally got up around 07:30 to find we were out to sea with the swell as high as our main deck. There was no way we were having lectures that morning. Nope. Not happening. I was feeling OK in my bed lying down, but once I stepped outside my cabin and walked up the stairs to the wheelhouse, the seasickness instantly hit. I grabbed an apple because I knew I was going to need something in my stomach in case of needing to bring that something back up through my system. Yes, I was preparing myself to throw up. Another skill I didn't know I would ever need.

The best thing to do in a situation like that was to go outside to get fresh air and to look at the horizon. My decision about not having lectures was instantly confirmed to be a good one when I opened the door of the wheelhouse to join a line of people already on the side of the deck in the same ill state as me.

It was time to fight the sea.

Tamara had previously taught me well that sometimes, it's

best to turn seasickness into a game, or rather – a battle. A battle between you and the sea. That often involved some yelling, but mostly willpower. The winner of the battle was determined by my ability, or inability, to not throw up, to hold it in. If I managed to keep it in, I would win and get a point. If I lost all control and the contents of my stomach, the sea got a point. (Which, when you think about it, wouldn't the sea lose when your vomit was suddenly spreading throughout it because that's rather disgusting?)

We passed around a box of corn flakes between us to try to calm our stomachs and focus on something else. Despite my best efforts, I succumbed to the reality that I was probably going to lose, and it was going to happen soon. I knew it was inevitable. I could feel the odds stacked against me, so I stood up in preparation for defeat, or rather surrender. Standing at the railing of the port quarter, I made the mistake of looking down at the water, and my eye caught sight of someone else's defeat. That did me in.

I lost.

Despite how much it sucks to throw up, it's still rather a refreshing experience when it's finished. Somehow.

I re-joined the battle line and restocked on cornflakes to replace those just lost. For a quick moment, I was feeling OK enough to attempt the journey back down to my bed. I lay flat on my back, eyes closed, and relief came. I managed to get a few hours' sleep before waking up to find the boat had stilled completely which was weird and unexpected but extremely welcome. We were finally in a safe, calm port, just not where I thought we'd be. We took refuge in Termini, a coastal town just north of Cefalù.

That afternoon, a couple crew members made a friend in town who agreed to drive them back down to Cefalù so they could assess the damage. We had ditched all of our mooring lines in our quick effort to get out of the harbour. It had been far too dangerous for someone to be out on the dock to release them with any hope of getting back on the ship. They found our mooring lines scattered all over the quayside but all still intact.

They secured the lines to the dock so we could easily grab them on our way through on a later day. Then, they went to check out the condition of the dinghy. That poor dinghy had been tied to another pontoon when the weather turned on us. There was no way of rescuing it when we left. We all had little hope for its survival anyways because we knew deep down the unlikelihood of that. The dinghy was devastatingly beyond repair. They took a picture of how they found it, and it was too upsetting for me to even look at. One side had a huge tear in it and was full of water, leaving it half-sunk in the harbour. The outboard motor was completely submerged and flooded. That dinghy and I had become really great friends, having some of the greatest adventures together. Seeing it in that state and completely beyond repair hurt my heart. At least we got to have one last great adventure together before it met its end.

We stayed in Termini for a day or two, waiting out the weather. After lunch on that Monday, we started making our way back to Cefalù, and luckily, the sun was shining, there was only a light breeze and the swell had subsided. It only took a few hours, so we were there before dinnertime. It was significantly calmer this time around, which was a relief. We were able to get the gangway out easily, and people could go ashore to enjoy the town that night. Cefalù really is a cool little town, and I wish we could have stayed there longer had the harbour been a bit nicer and more welcoming ...

It was 03:00 and I was awoken, yet again, by that freaking engine. I was confused because it felt relatively calm, so I couldn't understand why the engine was turning on, and I was fearful we were going to have to go out again. It was only on for a short time, so that was a relief as I had to get up two hours later. I still have no idea what had happened that caused them to do that, but it got my heart rate up. I slept terribly that night, waking up every forty-five minutes out of fear of missing my alarm for 05:00. Jo had to make her way back to Catania Airport, so it was an early morning for both of us; I wanted to go with her to make sure she got to where she needed to go. Our journey would be the opposite of when we first came there, but I wouldn't be going all the way to Catania with her this time. We set off at 05:30. As we left, I could feel the wind and swell slowly picking up once again, so I started wondering if it was going to be another fun adventure getting back to the ship later. Somewhat ignoring that because I had somewhere to be and it was still early in the morning and I am not fully functional at that time of day, I carried on.

We walked through the dark, quiet town with the sound of the rolling suitcase bumping along the cobblestone streets. We took the train to Palermo where I dropped Jo off and made sure she caught her bus to the airport. For me, it was back on the train to Cefalù.

I was pretty tired, so I enjoyed the quiet moment to just sit on the train and not have anything to do or anyone to talk to. An introvert needs her space sometimes. Well, a lot of times. That quiet moment ended quickly when I disembarked the train to a phone call.

'Hello?'

'Kellie! Where are you?'

'I just got off the train. I'm walking back through town to the ship right now.'

'OK, well, you need to hurry.'

'Everything OK? What's going on?'

'We just need you back as soon as possible.'

'Alright, I'll be there as soon as I can.' I started to walk a bit faster.

My earlier concerns proved to be true.

Racing through town, I made it down through the marina to the sight of the ship rocking and rolling similarly to the first time I walked through that marina, only it was daytime, and it wasn't raining. I had to make the big leap to get up onto the gangway that was hovering several feet above the quayside and hoist myself up. Right when I stepped foot on deck, they started bringing the gangway in behind me. They had already done all the other prep for sea so they were just waiting on me. Sure glad they waited.

We set sail for Messina in a hurry.

An hour later, I was due to be on watch from 12:00–16:00. Having already been up since 05:00 and navigating public transportation then rushing back to the boat to leave fast, I was tired. But such was life on a boat. Always unexpected, often inconvenient, but never boring. You just had to go with it.

It was a very uneventful sail, which I was happy about at that point. The wind picked up quite a bit in a few places, but we mainly kept the sails down and just headed for our destination. Being on the 00:00–04:00/12:00–16:00 watch kind of messes with your sleep schedule. And by kind of, I mean completely. Right after dinner, I went to sleep so I could be at least a little bit rested for my midnight watch. I was in a deep sleep when my alarm rudely woke me up at 23:30.

It was a quiet watch full of popcorn in the middle of the night. Popcorn was always a good companion on a sail. I took a minute to step outside on deck to check things out, and what should welcome me but my favourite constellation, Orion, along with the series of other stars I had come to be familiar with. Orion always seemed to show up in the moments I needed him most. In the moments of being worn out and tired, seeming to just push through life, he shows up and I smile and know it's going to be OK.

I don't even remember my head hitting the pillow after that watch.

Pumpkin

DATE: *November 2014*
LOCATION: *Termini, Sicily*
37° 59' 10.2" N
13° 42' 26.9" E

In the middle of all the unexpected changes and adventures that week comes another story, two years in the making.

One tradition I have had in my life for as long as I can remember has been carving pumpkins for Halloween. As October approached back in 2012, I hadn't thought I would be able to carry on this tradition as I didn't imagine there were many places in England, or Wales (where I would be), selling pumpkins.

I thought wrong.

While we were in Cardiff, I was taking a trip to the local Sainsburys and what should I see right as I walk in the door but a very large bucket full of baby pumpkins. I was shocked and so excited. I went back to the ship to tell Tamara about my excellent find. We devised this perfect plan that we'd carve the pumpkins, and then on the next sail, climb up to the top of the crow's nest and throw them into the sea. (Somewhat reminiscent of a certain Canadian Thanksgiving adventure I had the year prior when we carved pumpkins in a parking lot in the Canadian wilderness, got into an air tram and threw our pumpkins out the window down a 500-foot gorge.)

Pumpkins were purchased and we each had to secure them well in our cabin so that while we were sailing to Glasgow, they wouldn't fall and crash and splatter all over our room and ruin our plan.

They made it through the sail intact.

Everyone was watching a movie one night, so we took full advantage of having an empty galley to use as our carving station. We took our time drawing out what we were going to carve to make a masterpiece out of these pumpkins. We had sticky notes, a pen, a couple decent knives and some of Tamara's sharp art utensils for details, so we were ready.

It was a welcome surprise when both our pumpkins had plenty of seeds for roasting later. We cleaned out the goop and began carving. We lived on a ship where there was a rule on board of not having any open flames which meant no candles. (Unless it was for a birthday cake and you held a fire extinguisher right next to the person blowing the candle out just in case.) But what's a carved pumpkin if you can't light it up at night? We found our little electric tea candles, closed the door, and turned the lights off to get the full effect of our work.

Job well done.

The next task was to throw them into the ocean from the top of the crow's nest on the next sail, which was scheduled for a few days later. However, since we got stuck in Glasgow a whole lot longer than originally planned, the pumpkins decided to start rotting in the frigid cold of winter in Scotland. We disappointingly resorted to just throwing them into the rubbish. A bit anticlimactic.

Fail number one. But I guess there was always next year.

Well, the next year came ...

It was October 2013, and Tamara and I started planning how we could make attempt number two of our brilliant plan a success. Before I even had time to go searching for a pumpkin in Falmouth, England, I had come back to my cabin one night to find a perfect little pumpkin nestled by the pillow on my bed.

With a big smile on my face, knowing who was responsible for such a great little surprise, I walked out to the saloon, found Daniel and Tamara sitting behind one of the tables and exclaimed, 'There's a pumpkin on my bed!' They just smiled in response.

Several others joined us this year as Tamara and I created our own adorable Minion pumpkins. We took over the galley with pumpkin guts scattered over every counter. Thomas blew us all away with his 'Bean Harpooning a Shark' creation. He said he had never carved a pumpkin before, but I didn't believe him.

Our plan this time was to find a nice, sunny moment on our sail into the Med to throw them off the crow's nest. But the weather would not cooperate and was a bit of a rough journey with, you know, avoiding hurricanes. We had to secure our pumpkins in the skansen for days. The skansen was one of my favourite rooms in the whole ship but can get a little stuffy in there, especially when the fire door is closed and latched.

Once again, our pumpkins rotted. Squashed.

Fail number two.

So finally, in October 2014, the time was fast approaching to carve another pumpkin and attempt to actually be successful in throwing it off the crow's nest. I was determined to make this happen despite the absence of one vital piece – a Tamara – but also in the presence of a man who I knew wouldn't be happy with me if I threw anything overboard. That man was captain at the time, but it wasn't Captain Jeremy. Captain Jeremy probably would have come up with a better, much cooler plan.

The tricky part was that Halloween wasn't really a thing in Sicily. Pumpkin patches aren't common there. By the grace of God, I somehow managed to find some form of pumpkin in Sciacca at the price of only three euros. I was content, and the plan was in motion.

I had to take my next steps carefully as to when the carving would happen. I didn't want the same fails from the previous two attempts.

My plan was to carve the pumpkin when we got to Palermo. Then, I was going to throw it overboard on our sail to Cefalù. But if you'll remember ... I didn't get to go on that sail from Palermo to Cefalù. Instead, I spent the day on buses and trains and risked not getting back on board that night because of that stupid storm. With every delay leading up to it, my hope of this happening dwindled significantly. And with all the craziness our Cefalù adventures brought, I just knew it wasn't going to happen. My pumpkin was already rotting, as adorable as he might have been at first. I had given him a home on the shelf above my feet in my bunk to make sure he was safe and secure during the sail. One night I noticed some white stuff growing in one eye and in the side of his mouth. I took the lid off to a smell so awful that I knew it was time to dispose of it despite the lack of epicness with which to do so. But how, was the question. I didn't want to just throw it in a trash bag and bring it to the dumpster. That would just be boring and lame and the same thing I always did. I couldn't bring myself to succumb to a third failure in similar manner.

I had brought it out on deck and a few others were up there and they could see me debating what to do. Anthony encouraged me to still throw it overboard. Just in the marina this time. My rule-following-self warned him that I didn't want to do that seeing how the captain would clearly hear a splash from his cabin then would come out extremely disappointed and upset and probably mad for what we had done. I have never been one to put myself in any situation that could result in my getting in trouble. Though thinking back, I should have just done it.

But Anthony was as determined as I had been to make this happen. We just had to get creative. His idea was to put the pumpkin in a bucket, lower it down to the water and let it out. While it wasn't quite the same as throwing it to get the big splash, I agreed it was better than just dumping it in the trash. I hesitantly agreed after he had already run to get the bucket.

We plopped the pumpkin in the bucket, a perfect fit, and started lowering it. I continued to exclaim my worries to which Anthony's reply was that he could just say we were cleaning off the leftover vomit that was lingering on the aft ledge of the ship from earlier. This was something that legitimately needed to be done, so it was a sound excuse.

As the bucket made it to the water level, we realised it was going to be a bit harder than we thought to actually do this. The bucket wasn't easily tipping over to release the pumpkin. We had to swing the bucket back and forth with enough force for it to land sideways so it could actually fill up with water. This made the loud splashes I was afraid of. Then, as the bucket was finally full of water, I realised that pumpkins do not, in fact, sink. They definitely just float. Quite nicely, actually, but that wasn't exactly the goal. It was just lingering on the surface staring back at me, though still very much stuck in the bucket. More loud splashes and manoeuvring were required until it finally was loose in the harbour to which my concern continued to escalate. It was still floating. I had hoped it would fill with water and start sinking, but he just happily bobbed up and down right next to us.

Worst-case scenarios started racing through my mind as I thought about the captain coming out and seeing it and not being happy, and then the port authorities, who probably don't do carved pumpkins, seeing it and putting the pieces together that it probably came from that boat full of young people.

We lifted the bucket back up, full of water, and Anthony went on to clean the vomit off that ledge. If we were going to come up with a lie for getting away with tossing a pumpkin overboard, we might as well just do the thing. As he did this, who should come out to see what was going on but the captain.

He came over to us and quickly asked, 'What are you all doing? What's with the splashing back there?'

Immediately I responded back, 'Oh, Anthony and I were just cleaning up the side of the ship. There was a bunch of vomit still on it from earlier today.'

No lies there. Anthony was behind me diligently splashing off people's defeat, bless him.

The captain and I stood there conversing for a bit. My insides racing. As he talked to me, I kept glancing to the left just behind his shoulder to see the pumpkin slowly floating further and further away. I was paying very little attention to what he was saying as I kept stealing glances. I was hoping against hope that he wouldn't see it, and it would eventually float out of sight. The dang thing just wouldn't sink. I had to keep the conversation going until it was far enough away that I didn't think he'd notice.

'Welp, I'm going to go back inside now. Goodnight!'

I quickly passed him by and jetted down to my cabin.

Once inside, I laughed a nervous laugh, desperately hoping no one else would see it floating outside. I went back out about an hour later and it was gone. We never heard anything from port authorities though I'm still not entirely sure our captain didn't see it. I admit I was probably being quite dramatic about the whole thing. It was just a pumpkin in the water after all. No harm done.

I never did get to throw a pumpkin off the crow's nest which I'm still a little upset about. But the next year, when I was back home in Colorado, I climbed up the tree in my parents' front yard and threw a pumpkin out of it to make up for my three failed attempts, though my mom wasn't too thrilled with that idea. My original idea had been throwing it from the roof ...

Maybe one day ...

Give Me Something to Say

DATE: November 2014
LOCATION: Catania, Sicily
37° 29' 54.7" N
15° 5' 55.7" E

After our days going back and forth between Palermo and Termini and Cefalù, we made our way around Sicily to Catania. Our days in Catania were quite full. From the already busy DTS schedule we had, and climbing volcanoes, there was also a man who lived in Catania planning outreach opportunities for us. Every day for our first week there, we had visitors come on board periodically throughout the day – lectures being interrupted by loud Italian men getting a tour of the ship. It always proved for interesting encounters with someone from another culture and language who just showed up on our doorstep.

One night, with very little notice, we found out a youth group would be coming on board. There was not the best communication between our contact and the crew and among the crew themselves as to how this evening was going to look, so we just had to wing it. I was in a meeting in the Nav office with the rest of the DTS staff when Anthony burst in the door saying there were a whole lot of people down in the saloon, and he had no idea what to do. Meeting was over.

I rushed downstairs to find over thirty unfamiliar young faces filling every inch of the saloon in addition to our community of twenty-five or so scattered throughout. I immediately took charge, trying to figure out who the leader of this group was and what they were wanting to do. I eventually found him in the middle of this sea of people, and he gave me a bit of a rundown of his plan. I just went with it and said, 'OK, sure.' I had finally learned how to just go with the flow and change direction at a moment's notice. Too many plot twists in your life will do that to you.

In his rundown, he made quick mention of one of us giving some sort of speech/teaching/preaching to everyone. I did the simple smile-and-nod technique while in my mind I was kind of panicking. Suddenly, with only a few minutes to prepare, I had to give a message to a group of people I had never met who suddenly filled the spaces of my home. Cool.

They had brought a guitar and a few prepared worship songs in Italian to begin the evening. During those songs, I had a quick, stern little conversation with God.

'OK, God, I know that I'm going to have to give some sort of talk about something meaningful in a few minutes. Please give me a story to tell. A story with a good message that would be good for all these people to hear. Please give me something to say.'

He immediately came through and reminded me of a story I could tell. The story of not giving up on the first watch.

I began by telling them the story of my first experience as a watch leader and how I just wanted to give up. But it was only the first watch; I had to keep going, I had to push through because I was needed and there would be more watches to come. It was a story of not giving up. That pushing through is worth it.

They seemed to respond well in between the pauses of my words being translated. I hope that story meant something to someone in that room that night.

But it was one of those moments of seeing God come through right when I needed him to and reminding me of how far I had come. He did that often, and I was seeing the frequency of him doing that more and more every day.

By the Breakwater

DATE: December 2014
LOCATION: Catania, Sicily
$37°\ 29'\ 1.7"\ N$
$15°\ 5'\ 58.8"\ E$

In the summer of 2005, I was on a cruise in Alaska. One night, I went out to the balcony of my room because I had just read a paragraph from a book called *Blue Like Jazz* by Donald Miller that said he could feel God in the wind. I wanted to feel it. I walked through the door to the balcony and looked to my left. I felt the wind on my face and then I saw it.

I saw the brightness of the moon filling the night sky with its long and beautiful reflection on the water pointing right at me.

In that moment, I knew God's love, like, really knew it. I saw it, I felt it. I knew he loved me, and I knew I loved him. That moment stuck with me, buried deep beneath every other hurt and struggle and just life thrown on top over the years. That moment and that sight stuck with me and has always been a moment I think back on.

In the summer of 2013, I was at my friend Kara's house on the porch swing in her backyard enjoying the Colorado sunshine. She was telling me a story of how they got their house. They had sat down with their little girl and asked what she wanted their new house to have as they began looking. She said she wanted there to be a playground. So, they prayed and asked God for a house with a playground (among other things, I'm sure). God answered their prayer, and they got a beautiful house with a playground. God gave them what they asked for.

Kara had this view of God as a loving God. The kind of God who listens and hears what we want and gives it when we ask and believe. A good God. As she was telling me this story, I found myself getting so upset. I didn't see God that way then. I couldn't. I was hurting and confused, and it was hard for me to see God as good during that season of life.

What I didn't know was that day in Kara's backyard started me on a journey of seeking to know God as a loving God – seeing his goodness and love and faithfulness in everything. I was deeply desperate for it. But I had no idea how to get to that point. I couldn't understand the purpose of why the heck God wanted me to be on a ship because that ship was often hard to be on.

The next year or so that followed, I felt like I kept getting further and further away from what I was desperately searching for, further and further from seeing and knowing God's goodness. I went through storm after storm, squall after squall (both literal and figurative), close friends coming and going, stressful situations, feeling stuck, being thrown into things unprepared and unsupported, financially unstable. At times I wasn't happy. There was little joy, little peace; I couldn't see any goodness in it. I was hurt, confused and disappointed. And when you're seasick, as I've said before, everything sucks. I kept asking myself what in the world living on a boat had to do with anything in my life.

So, in the winter of 2014, I was on a boat in Sicily. It was nearing the end of my commitment to Next Wave. One dark night, I went for a run along the breakwater[27] and as I came to the end of it, I looked up. I saw a glimmer of the light of the moon slowly rising above the horizon, hiding behind the low

---

27 This is a section at the entrance of the harbour which literally breaks the water so it's calm inside the harbour. Often made of really big rocks piled up.

clouds. I sat by the water and watched it rise above those clouds until it came into full view.

I saw the brightness of the moon filling the night sky with its long and beautiful reflection on the water pointing right at me.

In that moment, I got it.

All the pieces were suddenly put together.

I saw him as a loving and good God. I could see it. I could feel it. I knew it. I knew it like that night in Alaska. I knew it like Kara knew it.

I saw the point and purpose in it all.

God had remembered that moment from nearly ten years before when the moonlight reflecting on the water did something in my heart. He knew what that meant to me. And he wanted to remind me not only that he remembered but that he was still the same God I could feel in the wind.

If the only purpose of the two years that I spent on that ship, all the storms and struggles and adventures, was to invite me in to see God as a loving God, it has been completely worth it.

I got to end on a good one.

Part 5
TO GRATITUDE

Remember my love on the waters
Before it all began
Before the anchor raised
Before you felt the sea swell beneath your feet
Before you took the helm
Before it all began
Remember my love on the waters

Remember my love on the waters
In the midst of it all
In the midst of the storm
In the midst of the darkness
In the midst of the fear
In the midst of it all
Remember my love on the waters

Remember my love on the waters
After it came to an end
After passing by the breakwater
After the lines secured
After standing still on solid ground
After it came to an end
Remember my love on the waters

Remember my love on the waters
For I have been good to you

The Last Sail

DATE: December 2014
LOCATION: Blue Lagoon, Comino, Malta
   36° 0' 49.8" N
   14° 19' 23.5" E

We had made our back to Gozo after circumnavigating Sicily. It was one of those moments that felt like coming home when pulling back in to Mgarr Marina. It was the last day of lectures and Captain Jeremy (who was back on board with us by this point) wanted to go for one more short sail to the Blue Lagoon. Preparations were made, and as lectures began, lines were cast off on deck and we headed out of the marina towards the island of Comino – a small island between Malta and Gozo with a local population of four. Yes. Just four. I walked by their house. (It was also a filming location for the 2002 movie, *Count of Monte Cristo*, the exteriors of a tower on a hill being used as the Château d'If prison ...) During the summer season, that population grows exponentially as it is a very popular tourist destination with hiking trails throughout the hills and lawn chairs lining what little space there is next to the water.

The Blue Lagoon gets its name from the unique blueness of the water. It is a colour not found in many places. During the winter months, like December, no one is there (except the four that actually reside there), so we had the whole lagoon to ourselves. Next Wave took up the vast majority of space there anyway.

By the time morning tea break came around, I went up on deck to find us anchored to the seabed which was just a few metres beneath the bottom of our hull. Zhenya and Kyrah were already in the water helping steady us by doing something creative that Captain Jeremy came up with. He did that often, always coming up with interesting systems that actually worked incredibly well. It was slightly windy and cold and there were storm clouds in the distance, but I was determined to swim. I knew this would be my last chance to jump off Next Wave into the Mediterranean Sea. And what better place to do that than the Blue Lagoon? We had some lunch, and then the swimming preparations began. The ladder was out on the side, ready to be climbed up by swimmers who were brave enough to take the chilly plunge.

We all lined up along the ledge on the outside of the ship, holding onto the rail behind us waiting for everyone to be ready for the great leap. We counted off and all jumped in unison. What a great and refreshing feeling to one moment be flying through the air and the next be completely surrounded by the bluest of blue water. But it was freaking cold. The kind of cold that takes your breath away and makes you numb. After a short while, I got used to it and just enjoyed feeling the sunshine on my face and remembering how much I loved and had missed swimming in the sea. Having spent a hot summer swimming in the Med every day, this was just a bit different but still so great to be able to float effortlessly and swim through the smoothness of the salty water. But after about ten minutes or so, it was time to get out. It was too cold to handle for a long time, and I was starting to go completely numb all over.

After drying off, we started hoisting the anchor to head back over to Gozo. I knew I needed to get to Captain Jeremy and quick. I had a really important question to ask him, and I didn't want anyone else to beat me to it.

I raced from the foredeck towards the wheelhouse and called out to Captain Jeremy.

'Hey, Jeremy!'

'Yes?'

'Would it be alright if I could helm us back into Gozo?'

'Of course! Get behind the wheel, let's be on our way.'

I took my favourite perch behind the helm, ready to steer us out of the Blue Lagoon and back into Mgarr Marina. I wouldn't realise the even greater significance of this opportunity to helm until we were halfway across the way to Gozo.

I waited at the helm for Captain Jeremy's orders to make our way. I heard the clunk of the anchor hitting the hull, locked in place, followed by a thumbs up from Kyrah in the bow signalling the anchor being secure. Jeremy set the pitch to full ahead, turned up the revs of the engine, and told me to head straight towards the marina.

There is something really special to me about helming. There always had been. Ever since the first moment when Tamara passed the course to me, and I took the wheel for the first time in the English Channel, it was always my absolute favourite thing to do. And frankly, something I was actually really good at. I've done it in so many different circumstances, places and weather conditions. Every time I got behind the wheel, it steered just a little bit different, so I'd have to work with the swell and the waves and the wind and discover how the boat would react to the number of times I turned the wheel. When being in control of a 42-metre, 199-tonne, million British Pound Sterling yacht, there's a lot of responsibility and respect that floods my veins at the helm but in the best of ways.

A cardinal buoy, or cardinal mark, is a buoy in the water which indicates the position of something hazardous, whether shallow water or jagged rocks or the like. There are four different cardinal buoys – north, south, east and west. These buoys have markings that tell you which direction of the buoy to keep to in order to avoid that hazard. They tell you where safe waters are. These markings are indicated in three different ways: two cones on top pointing in varying directions, a distinctive pattern of yellow and black stripes along the buoy, and a sequence of flashing lights.

For example, a west cardinal buoy would have the two cones pointing towards each other at the very top, a colour pattern going down of yellow, black, yellow, and a flash of light nine times every fifteen seconds. These buoys are also marked on navigational charts. If they were shown on the chart to be along our intended course, it was the duty of the watch to look out for them and be sure we kept to the appropriate direction and distance from them.

As odd as it might sound, I loved finding these cardinal buoys. I would scan the chart for when we were to pass by one on our course and get excited when we had to be on the lookout for them. I always wanted to be the first to spot it and confirm which one it was. If it was night and I'd see a light flashing in the distance, I'd stand still (well, as still as I was able) with my eyes focused straight on it, counting every flash of light and the time between them to make sure it was the buoy I was looking for. No matter how many times I confirmed it was indeed the cardinal buoy mapped on the chart, I'd still keep counting every flash until it was out of sight.

They showed us the way to go, day or night.

I had learned to look for them, learned to recognise them, learned to use them to direct my way.

About halfway on our journey from Comino to Gozo, sitting in my favourite spot in the wheelhouse with my left arm up on the railing next to me, my left foot resting up on the rail beneath that, my right hand on the helm, I looked to my left out the window. The sight I saw was the deep blue sea and the light blue sky above it with the sun shining beautifully and sparkling along the surface of the water as we moved through it. In that moment, I realised how much I was going to miss that view. This was going to be my very last sail on Next Wave, and it was starting to hit me. Thinking back to all the times I've helmed and all the times I looked out that window and all the different scenes I'd seen through it, I couldn't help but get sentimental at the thought of this being my last time to look through that window to the open waters beyond it.

Then, something happened which added to the sentimentality of that moment and nearly made me cry. A west cardinal buoy passed next to us in the distance on our port side, standing tall in the water right in the middle of that window. It was too perfect a sight to have planned for.

I thought back to everywhere I had been, every person I had met, every adventure I'd had. Every piece. I remembered the storms, the sunrises, the sunsets, the stars. I had learned and experienced so much, and it all came flooding back in an instant.

After a few minutes of staring through the window remembering everything, after the buoy was out of sight, I looked back to the bow and realised I was getting rather off course. Captain Jeremy looked back at me wondering what I was doing to be getting so off our heading. I snapped back into the present moment and refocused my attention ahead of us, though I still stole glances of the sea through the window next to me.

After some fancy manoeuvring by the brilliant Captain Jeremy in the marina to avoid being run over by a massive ferry coming towards us, we were moored along the quayside in Gozo once again.

I lingered at the helm for a few minutes after our mooring lines were secure and everyone had left the wheelhouse. A wave of gratitude flowed through me.

I was grateful to had helmed my last sail.

The Nickey Line

DATE: March 2011
LOCATION: Harpenden, England
51° 49' 29.3" N
0° 21' 34.6" W

I had never been a big runner most of my life. When I was in high school, I remember driving to school and I'd see runners running through the cold snow, and I thought they were crazy. I never understood why people wanted to run at all let alone long distances in freezing temperatures. But then I did it once and kind of liked it, and then I became one of those people I always thought was crazy running through the snow.

Going back to the very first week I was in England for my DTS in 2011, I met Catherine. She introduced me to hot squash and flapjacks and would become an incredible mentor to me. She also liked running. I wanted to like running more, and I wanted to run with her because I thought she was really cool and I wanted to spend more time with her. So, I started running. I would go on short little runs around town, nothing too extravagant, but all the while having the desire to run with Catherine as my motivation.

One morning, I surprised myself and ran around The Oval nine times before breakfast. Three times around The Oval is roughly equal to a mile. So that was three miles I did in about half an hour, without stopping. It was the best run I had ever done up to that point. I felt like I was ready to take on a run with the amazing Catherine. So, we started running together. We ran about twice a week in the cold, early mornings. Sometimes in gorgeous weather but most times through thick mud which then stuck to the bottom of our shoes making me a couple inches taller, with the wind and rain pounding our faces.

One Saturday morning, Catherine and I went for a long run. I was unaware at the start just how long the run was going to be, but I always just went where Catherine led on our runs. She knew those fields better than I did, and I was grateful she took me along. She had a loop she would go on which started at the beloved Nickey Line just outside the gates of YWAM Harpenden, cut through different pathways leading through endless fields, a quick jaunt in a small, wooded area, around the top of Rothamsted Park, back around some more fields, meeting back up with The Nickey Line again to head back to the bridge where we started. (This was the loop I made a map of from memory ...).

The sun was shining beautifully that morning (which was rare), and we were running through the open fields and through the woods. It was hard though. She had a bit of a faster pace than what I was comfortable with, so I had to push hard to keep up, and I was getting tired.

About halfway through, having had a painful stitch in my side for most of our run, through heavy breaths, I finally gave in and asked, 'Hey, could we stop and walk for just a minute?'

I was not expecting her to respond as she did.

'Really? Are you sure?'

I glanced over at her without saying a word, not liking that she didn't want to let me stop.

'Do you really want to stop?' she asked again.

I'm not sure whether it was my competitive nature that kicked in or a sudden onset of determination but through another heavy breath I huffed, 'No.'

So, we kept running. I pushed through the pain and awful stitch in my side to get to the end. I kept going no matter how tired I was, no matter how much I wanted to stop, no matter how appealing giving up sounded.

Catherine always liked to sprint to the end on our runs. This was a habit I joined her with on our shorter runs but not something I could commit to on this one. As she sprinted on ahead of me, I was even more determined to keep my pace. I saw the bridge which marked the end of our route in the distance, and I looked straight ahead as it drew closer with every tired step. I was almost there. Catherine was waiting for me at the end, and I had to keep going. Stopping now would be defeat.

I made it to the bridge and finally stopped to catch my breath. I limped over to Catherine and gave her a sweaty and likely unwanted hug, but I didn't care. It was just the absolute best feeling to have finished, to have run the entire 5.6 miles, and to share that victory with her. At that point, that was the farthest I had ever run in one go, and I was amazed at having accomplished it.

Catherine challenged me that day. She allowed me to discover that I was capable of pushing through no matter how much it hurt, no matter how hard it was, no matter how inadequate I felt. She knew I could do it. (Well, that or she just really didn't want to stop to walk herself ... maybe a bit of both? Either way, it was a meaningful moment, and I'm glad she didn't let me stop.)

I've gone on to run four half marathons so far, which have been amazing accomplishments I'm so incredibly proud of. (And no, I have no desire to run a full marathon, so you don't even need to ask ...) But that first 5.6-mile run with Catherine will always be special to me. It will always be the one I think back on to give me that push to finish.

Whenever I want to quit, whether on a run or even in life, I hear Catherine answering my question with another question of 'Really? Are you sure? Do you really want to stop?' And in turn I can respond, 'No!'

That run that one Saturday morning showed me that I am the kind of person who pushes through when things get hard. I had been told that before, but this run finally allowed me to see it in myself. And it's that which set the foundation and gave me the drive and determination I needed to keep going and not give up in the storms, not give up when things got hard when living on a boat. There is this motivation that comes, knowing that I can accomplish whatever comes my way. A knowing I have seen played out over and over through the course of my time and crazy adventures on S/Y Next Wave and beyond.

And it started when Catherine wouldn't let me quit on a run.

Remembering a Yes

DATE: March 2015
LOCATION: Harpenden, England
          51° 49' 29.3" N
          0° 21' 34.6" W

I went up to the office in the Clock Building on Highfield Oval in Harpenden, England after the DTS had finally graduated and it was finished. I had to pay my final crew fees and officially end my time with Next Wave and with YWAM. A bit of a bittersweet moment.

Two and a half years before, I had asked God in a boiler room if I should to the STCW training course, the training needed to be a qualified crew member. The deal was that if I did the course, I could pay it off with time served on Next Wave. If I served twenty-four months in total, it would be completely paid off. If I did less than that, I'd have to pay back the difference. At that point, in the beginning, it made no sense for me to do it. I was only planning to be on the boat for six months, and I certainly didn't have that kind of money to pay it back.

But God's yes was immediate when I asked him.

We were looking through my account to be sure everything was finalised. At this point, I started to get worried about how much I was going to owe for that STCW. With some of the breaks I had taken off the ship, I wasn't sure if I made it to that twenty-four-month mark. I had so little left in my bank account from paying off my crew fees that I was panicking at what else I owed.

But then I was told that the cost of my STCW was completely covered. To the day. I had served exactly twenty-four months to the ministry of S/Y Next Wave.

I was so relieved as I walked out of the Clock Building. I remembered God's yes when I asked him about this all those years before.

He knew.

He flipping knew.

He knew the adventures ahead and wanted me to be as prepared as I possibly could be for whatever came my way.

Because that's the kind of God he is. The kind that is good and loving and faithful. That kind that invites us into every season of our lives, good or bad, easy or hard, because he knows the good that's to come.

Guiding Hand of a Loving God

To be grateful for the good things that happen in our lives is easy, but to be grateful for all of our lives the good as well as the bad, the moments of joy as well as the moments of sorrow, the successes as well as the failures, the rewards as well as the rejections, that requires hard spiritual work. Still, we are only grateful people when we can say thank you to all that has brought us to the present moment. As long as we keep dividing our lives between events and people we would like to remember and those we would rather forget, we cannot claim the fullness of our beings as a gift of God to be grateful for. Let's not be afraid to look at everything that has brought us to where we are now and trust that we will soon see in it the guiding hand of a loving God.
~ Henri Nouwen

Coming to the end of a significant chapter prompts a lot of looking back, reflecting, reminiscing, remembering all the plot lines and characters and events that have made up the pages.

Despite its many challenges, its countless ups and downs, I see nothing but good and nothing but God in the story. I can look back to who I was when this all started and see how every part of it carried me to the next and transformed me to who I am now.

For a long time, I viewed God as one who took away from me the things I loved and led me to places I didn't want to be, forcing me to do hard things. I mean, it's true that God asks us to do hard things. But it took a whole lot of storms for me to realise that those hard things are always for our good and the good of those around us.

I can finally see that loving God they always talk about. I know it now and am forever grateful for it.

So, remembering back to that one night in Gozo, God knew what he was doing when he said I was going to know so much more of his goodness.

Remember the awesome chart puzzle I made? Well, I brought it back out during the final week of the DTS. It started with a puzzle, and I wanted it to end with one. But this time with a bit of a different meaning.

One of the most frustrating things in my life is when a puzzle is missing a piece. I could have put together 2,998 pieces of a 3,000-piece puzzle and been more upset about those two missing pieces than proud of the fact that I put together 2,998 tiny puzzle pieces. Yes, that actually happened. And I hated it. When I took a step back, all I could see were the missing pieces.

But that's because *every* piece is important. *Every* piece is necessary. *Every* piece is needed.

Every person, place, experience, storm, challenge, sunrise, sunset, line snapping, fear, glowing dolphin, movie night, galley dance party, rope swing, worship time, teaching, and throwing up over the rail. It was all part of a greater story God was writing with my life. Without one single piece, without one single story, the picture wouldn't be complete.

Every piece is a meaningful experience that has made me who I am today.

Every piece is important.
Every piece is necessary.
Every piece is needed.

And I'm forever grateful for every piece of the puzzle that is my life.

God invites us into the unknown, into the uncertainty, into the uncomfortable. He invites us to something new, to see and know him, to feel his absence, to find his redemption. And he invites us to gratitude for every part of it.

It's up to us to say yes and let God blow us away with the story he invites us to write with our lives.

Let us lift our eyes to the one who has called us here this night
Let us lift our voices to the one who has brought us this far
Let us lift our hands to the one who has made us who we are
Let us lift our hearts to the one who has made us his delight

Remember, O heart, the anticipation you felt
The day you left your home
Remember, O heart, the first time he met you
And the amount of love he dealt

Remember the fun, the joy, and the laughter
Remember the faces, the names you know
The places you visited
And the dreams you chased after

(Take a minute to remember these good things)

We give back to you, O Lord
The good times and the hard
We acknowledge you for how far we've come
For you are the one we have adored

Thank you for the mountains we climbed
Thank you for the oceans we sailed
Thank you for the seas we swam
Thank you for the stars we admired
Thank you for the miles we travelled
Thank you for the places we explored
Thank you for the friendships formed
Thank you for the hurt healed
Thank you for the hearts changed

May we remember your love, all our days
May your joy fill our hearts
May your blessing be upon us this night
May you receive all the glory, all the honour, and all the praise
Amen

A Liturgy by Daniel Jackson

Epilogue
Southampton

DATE: One September
LOCATION: Southampton, England
        50° 53' 47.2" N
        1° 24' 22.3" W

In September of 1964, my mom, along with her Mam and five of her six siblings, travelled south from Sunderland to Southampton to board the S.S. America which would take them across the Atlantic Ocean from England to New York. How my grandmother managed a week-long voyage with six children ranging from two to twelve years old through the stormy seas of the Atlantic, I'll never understand. What a strong and brave woman Grandma Bristow was. They had no idea what life awaited them as they embarked on a new adventure to America.

    In September of 2012, I travelled south from London to Southampton to board a ferry that would take me down the river to the Isle of Wight to board S/Y Next Wave, which would take me around the UK and through the entire length of the Mediterranean Sea. I hardly knew anyone, and I hardly knew what life awaited me as I embarked on a new adventure on a sailboat.

    My mom started something new from the port of Southampton, England, one September.

I also started something new from the port of Southampton, England, one September (just a few years later …).

I think it's funny when things like this come full circle. Some would say it's just a coincidence and think nothing of it. But I think it's another way God shows us who he is.

He knew that the journey my mom went on from England would mean something special to me. And he brought it around for me to experience as well, in my own way.

And at his invitation.

May you see and know the goodness and faithfulness of God in your life. Through the storms. Through the adventures. Through the doors God invites you to step through. May you walk through life knowing he is always with you and always for you. Knowing he is a God who keeps his promises. Knowing the deep love that he has for you. Knowing that he is good.

"...DON'T FORGET YOUR OLD SHIPMATES..."

Acknowledgements

Living on YWAM S/Y Next Wave was truly a once-in-a-lifetime opportunity. Words will never come close to accurately describing my gratitude. I mean, it was hard. It was a pressure cooker environment to live in. But it was also beautiful. I love that I get to look back at every moment, the good and the bad, with a smile on my face and gratitude in my heart for every single person I got to live with in community on that boat and the places I got to see. Getting the chance to write this book, to relive some of these experiences, has been such a blessing. And the contents of this book only cover a fraction of life on that boat.

    To Daniel and Tamara, thank you for taking a chance on some random person you hardly knew to let join your crew. You two are amazing and have truly made an inexpressible impact on my life. Thank you for your friendship and just being so cool. Tamara, thank you for teaching me how to helm and thank you for being a part of this project with me through your incredible artwork.

    To Mom and Dad, thank you for supporting me through all my crazy adventures. Thank you for always allowing me the space to do what was right for me and being behind me the whole time.

To Uncle Ed, thank you for encouraging me that if I was faithful to God in the small things, He would be faithful to me with the big things.

To my Panama House Family, thank you for encouraging and supporting the crap out of me through this entire book writing, editing and publishing process. Thank you for celebrating every single step with me.[28]

To Kara, thank you for being the first person in my life to see something greater in me that I didn't see in myself. You saw it, called it out and invited me into the opportunity to see it in myself. Without that influence, I'm not sure I would have ever been courageous enough to join crew on a boat in Europe.

To Amanda, thank you for encouraging me that these stories are worth telling for people to hear.

To Nicole, thank you for listening to me during a tough season in life and opening my eyes to the possibility that it might actually be an invitation to something new, something good. Because it absolutely was. And it led to so much of the inspiration for this book.

To Bethany, thank you for lending so much of your time and working so hard with your amazing attention to detail and incredible graphic design skills to help make the images in this book look even better.

To Scott and Jen, thank you for asking me to housesit and hang out with Otis in your gorgeous mountain home that provided the best space to write so much of this book.

To Atlas Coffees, thank you for appreciating good tea and being the perfect place to edit.

To Self-Publishing School, thank you for helping me make this dream of publishing a book a reality. And special thanks to

---

[28] A special footnote to say a special thanks to Shannon for the idea to use footnotes.

Barbara for coaching me through every step.

To my YWAM Harpenden community, now spread around the world, thank you for the part you play in my story. It's where it all started and I'm so grateful for that.

To Catherine, thank you for never letting me quit on a run.

To Thomas, thank you for the fantastic bean illustrations. The beans never fail to make me and everyone else smile.

To Brian and Anne, thank you for starting the ministry of YWAM Next Wave and so faithfully serving. My life is better for having been a part of it.

And the greatest of thanks to all my old Next Wave shipmates, there's a lot of you ... you know who you are. These stories would not be what they are without a single one of you in them, whether I sailed with you for a couple days or a couple years. Thank you for sharing life on a boat with me, even through the rough seas. I hope reading this book brought you back to those days spent on the sea and that you can see the goodness of it all in your own story.

About the Artist
Tamara Jackson

Tamara Jackson is an artist originally from Vancouver, Washington, in the USA but has made her home in Cuckfield, England since 2014. Since 2008 she has volunteered full time with Youth with a Mission, including several years on YWAM S/Y Next Wave. Creative practice has been central to sharing her faith, and that practice has been strongly influenced by Tamara's experience travelling and living internationally. She earned a distinction for her work in the Foundation in Art and Design course at Brighton Metropolitan College in 2018–2019. Tamara lives in England with her husband and young daughter.

Contact: tamarajacksonart@gmail.com
Instagram: @tamarajacksonart